STEP-BY-S

CP/M Plus On The Amstrad PCW

STEP-BY-STEP

CP/M Plus On The Amstrad PCW

John Campbell

NEW TECH

Newtech
An imprint of Butterworth-Heinemann Ltd
Linacre House, Jordan Hill, Oxford OX2 8DP

PART OF REED INTERNATIONAL BOOKS

OXFORD LONDON BOSTON
MUNICH NEW DELHI SINGAPORE SYDNEY
TOKYO TORONTO WELLINGTON

First published 1992
Reprinted 1992

© John Campbell 1992

All rights reserved. No part of this publication may be reproduced in any material form (including photocopying or storing in any medium by electronic means and whether or not transiently or incidentally to some other use of this publication) without the written permission of the copyright holder except in accordance with provisions of the Copyright, Designs and Patents Act 1988 or under the terms of a licence issued by the Copyright Licensing Agency Ltd, 90 Tottenham Court Road, London, England W1P 9HE. Applications for the copyright holder's written permission to reproduce any part of this publication should be addressed to the publishers

British Library Cataloguing in Publication Data
A CIP catalogue record for this book is available from the British Library

ISBN 0 7506 0460 3

Printed and bound in Great Britain by
Biddles Ltd, Guildford and King's Lynn

Contents

About this book

Foreword 3
Some groundwork 5
Looking after your discs 7
How to use this book 9

Chapter 1 First Steps

Introduction 13
What CP/M is and why you need it 14
The basic components of CP/M 17
What jobs can you do with CP/M? 18
Housekeeping tasks we shall examine 19
Making the computer do a series of jobs with one command 20
PROFILE.ENG or .SUB 22
Copying a file and giving the copy
a different name 24
Submitting a list of commands 26
Submitting PROFILE.SUB automatically 29
Erasing PROFILE.SUB 30
Using the RPED text editor 31

Contents

RPED - creating a new file............................. 34
RPED- editing an existing file........................ 37

Chapter 2 Managing Files

Naming and storing files................................ 43
Matching up file names ('masks')................... 45
Renaming a file... 47
Making a duplicate copy of a file..................... 49
The TYPE command 51
TYPE command - enhancements 52
A general note about commands 52
Using PIP – enhancements............................. 54
Copy several files with the similar names....... 54
Copy an ASCII file to the screen or printer 54
Sending information direct from
the keyboard to the printer 56
Sending information from
the keyboard to disc 57
Copying several files into one big one 58
Getting rid of unwanted files........................... 62
Protecting files -
Read Only 64
System files... 65
User numbers 67
Setting passwords... 69

Contents

Using SET on drives and discs 71
Setting the attributes of a disc drive 71

Chapter 3 Managing Discs

Checklist - looking after discs 77
Resetting (rebooting) the PCW 78
Creating a (data) disc 79
Booting automatically into a program 82
Editing PROFILE.SUB 86
Finding out what is on a disc 88
DIR variants (options) 90
Checking the space on a disc 96
SHOW - variants (options) 98
Making a duplicate copy of a disc 99
Note for PCW9512 users 99
PCW9512: copying a disc from 8000 format .. 103

Chapter 4 Managing Hardware

Setting the PCW's clock 109
Checking the PCW's clock 110
Putting screen and printer outputs
into disc files 111
Automating procedures with GET and
SUBMIT 116

Contents

Tweaking the screen... 121
PALETTE.COM.. 121
SET24X80... 122
The keyboard under CP/M Plus...................... 123
Using the NumLock function........................... 125
ALT or CONTROL codes 127
Control codes summary.................................. 128
Tweaking the keyboard................................... 129
The key definition file...................................... 130
Using the key definition file............................. 133
Tweaking the keyboard to streamline work..... 134
Loading new keyboard settings automatically. 139
A final word or two.. 141

Appendix A Using Other Printers

Appendix B Glossary

Index

About this book

Foreword

When I started writing this book I remember thinking to myself, 'Oh gawd! Why would anyone want to read a book about CP/M Plus, let alone write one!?' But the further I got into things and the more I jogged my memory about what you can do with CP/M, the more enthusiastic I became. If you have been using your PCW exclusively as a word processor or have been working only with the LocoMotive software packages, you may not realise that you have met CP/M Plus, so what is it? And why do you need it? And what use is it to you anyway!?

Well, these are the questions I try to answer in this book. Now I could do that by examining the components of the system to see what they do and how they work, but I think there is a better way to look at your computer system. I suspect that you, like me, don't actually care about what goes on under the bonnet. I suspect that you are far more interested in what you can make the PCW do for you. So, the whole approach of this book is, how you can achieve things with your PCW – how you can use its facilities to make your life easier. In fact, how you can use CP/M Plus to manage your work better. So, what is CP/M Plus?

Very briefly CP/M stands for Command Program for Microcomputers. It is the Operating System for your PCW (and a range of other '8 bit' computers). Stated baldly, an operating system (like CP/M Plus) is a computer program which controls or manages the way the computer, and all the other items of hardware linked to it, operate together as a single system. It enables the computer to 'talk' to the various bits which make up its own system, such as the printer and the screen and the keyboard, as well as enabling the computer to interact with the world outside its own system. It also enables you to control what the computer does.

Foreword

I wanted this book to be a practical guide – the sort of book I would have liked when I first started working with CP/M in the early days of 'micro-computers' (as they were called then). So, I have looked at the full range of CP/M's capabilities and I have tried to identify those features which the average PCW owner is likely to use. I applied Pareto's principle to judge which 20 percent of activities the average PCW user will carry out to get 80 percent of his or her results. And I have written about those features of CP/M Plus.

I have, therefore, not even attempted to answer every last question about CP/M Plus. I shall not, for example, be discussing the finer points of machine code programming – if you are at that stage, you can probably understand the manual in any case. No, I have tried to keep things simple and useful and I have tried to write a Step-By-Step guide that even I can understand.

It is up to you to judge if I have succeeded.

John Campbell
Tillington, Hereford. 1992

Some groundwork

You will know that when you work with a piece of software, such as LocoScript, you generate lots of files which themselves need working on from time to time. Some will become redundant and will need to be scrapped, others will need renaming, yet others will be on the wrong disc and so on. Keeping on top of these necessary, 'housekeeping' activities is a job in itself..

If you have read either of the Step-By-Step books, Using the PCW9512 or Exploiting the PCW9512, you'll know you can do many housekeeping jobs while LocoScript is running. But you'll also know that from time to time you may want to do several housekeeping jobs in one session – spring cleaning, if you like. When this happens, you will find it much quicker to do the jobs without starting up LocoScript first. In fact you will find it easier to do them using certain of the 'Utility' programs that come with CP/M Plus. So how do you get at CP/M Plus?

Your computer has at least one floppy disc drive built into it. It is through this disc drive that you feed information to the computer, once you have switched on the power. The first information you must give the computer is its operating system, CP/M.

If your work with the PCW has been limited, so far, to using LocoScript, you will know that all you have to do to start-up the system is, switch on the machine and then put the LocoScript disc into the A: disc drive. The PCW takes it from there to get LocoScript ready for you to use. Starting up under CP/M is just as easy.

Some groundwork

To start-up the PCW so you can work with CP/M, you simply use the disc labelled 'CP/M Plus' instead of the LocoScript disc. You will find that CP/M doesn't give you as much help as LocoScript does – in fact it hardly gives you any help at all – but that's what this book is for, so there's no problem.

Before we go any further, let me sound a note of caution. You should never use your master discs for everyday work. As soon as you get your PCW you should make duplicate, 'backup', copies of your master discs. (See the section in the book headed, 'Making a duplicate copy of a disc', if you don't know how to do it). Once you have your duplicates, put the masters away somewhere safe and use the duplicates as your 'working copies'.

I stress this point at the outset, because the PCW's discs seem quite hard and robust. It is easy to fall into the trap of thinking they are unbreakable. But believe me, a PCW's disc can be damaged – and you don't have to try too hard! For example, you can destroy months of work on a disc:

- by getting it too near to a magnetic field of some kind
- by spilling coffee on it
- by getting greasy fingerprints on the magnetic surface
- by formatting it when you thought you were copying it. (If you don't know what that means, read Chapter 3.)

Looking after your discs

There seems little point in taking great care of your files, if you are cavalier about handling the discs which hold the files. That's why I'm starting this book with a checklist of things we should all do to protect our discs.

Now you might perhaps think that the tips on the next page sound like the rantings of a neurotic, but that's probably because you've never been in the position of damaging a disc which holds several weeks, perhaps months, of work. Remember, the first rule of Murphy's law states: 'If a thing can go wrong it will.' But also remember that the second, and more worrying rule is, 'Things will go wrong at the worst possible time.'

When you kill a disc, and you experience that hot sick feeling, then you'll see what I mean. But then it will be too late. So, have a look at the checklist and then we can go on to look at various housekeeping procedures which will help you manage your files, your discs and your hardware, to stave off the onset and minimise the effects of Murphy.

Looking after your discs

- Make a back-up of a Program Disc as soon as you get it. **If you have not made copies of the PCW's master discs, do so now!**

- Work with your back-up discs not your master discs

- Once you start working with your PCW you will start to create data files. You should back-up those files, at the end of each working session at the very least

- If, during a working session, you create or edit several files, then back-up each file as soon as you finish working with it

- Always store master discs and back-ups in separate boxes, preferably in separate rooms. Always store discs in a dust proof container of some kind at room temperature

- Never touch the magnetic surfaces of the disc

- Never switch the computer on or off with a disc in a drive

- As a general rule, try to keep data files (the work you've done) on separate discs from programs (program files)

- Unless you need to save information on your program disc, it is a good idea to write protect it before you start work. Push the 'write protect tab' (in the top left hand corner of the disc) down towards the letter A or B

- Make sure that you establish a routine procedure for identifying discs (and what's on them) - an index of some kind.

How to use this book

This book is laid out in a particular way. Normal explanatory text, like this, is laid out so it extends to both margins of the page. When I am providing a list of items, such as:

- steps in a checklist

- alternative ways of doing things

- key elements of a problem

I use indented 'bullet points', as I have done here. But, of course, this is a Step-By-Step book, so I shall also be providing detailed instructions on how to carry out the various tasks we shall be examining. There are two things to notice here: Firstly every page has a header which will help you keep track of where you are. Secondly, each step in a procedure appears in a numbered, 'do-this' paragraph. For example:

CP/M Plus has a 'help facility' which you may like to use from time to time. This is how you use it.

1 Switch on your PCW and put a copy of your CP/M start-up disc in drive A:. Wait a few moments until the screen display settles down.

2 **If you have an 8000 series machine** (8256 or 8512), replace your start-up disc with a copy of disc 4, the one labelled, 'DR LOGO & HELP'.

3 Key-in: the word **HELP** and then tap the **{RETURN}** key.

9

How to use this book

The 'HELP' program will run and the screen will provide you with prompts on how to use it.

In that example of a typical procedure, there are a few of things to notice about 'do-this' paragraphs:

- When I want you to key-in something at the keyboard, the thing I want you to key-in appears **IN BOLD CAPITALS IN THIS TYPEFACE**, which is different from the normal one

- When I want you to tap the RETURN key, it appears like this: **{RETURN}**

- All the other special keys on the keyboard, such as **ALT, EXIT, EXTRA, SHIFT, SPACEBAR**, etc. appear as they do here

- Any special notes **are presented in this typeface**

Note

Sometimes, when we are working through a lengthy procedure, it involves two or three distinct sets of activities. In such cases you will find that the 'do-this' numbering starts at 1 for each set of activities. (From time to time I add extra information, which may not be immediately obvious from the text or activity which precedes it. When I do so, it is in the form of a note like this.)

So, having covered those details, it is time for you to read the book and work through the practical examples.

Chapter 1
First Steps

Introduction

Before we launch off into an exploration of the CP/M Plus operating system we had best be sure we have the same understanding of a few things. For a start, what is an operating system anyway ... and why do you need it.!?

So I want to take a short while to cover some essential concepts. I'll do this by posing some questions and then answering them. So, if you already know why you need CP/M and what it is, then please bear with me for a couple of pages.

What CP/M is and why you need it.

When you switch on your PCW, it is effectively brain-dead. The lights are on, but there's nobody in. Well, almost nobody. In fact there is a small spark of life that's wired-in permanently and its job is to prompt you to put a disc into the computer. Not just any old disc, though. Before the PCW can operate at all, it needs to have a program which tells it how to work. In other words, it needs an Operating Program, or an Operating System and it must be on the disc you use to start-up the computer.

On the PCW the operating system is CP/M Plus. Once you have supplied a suitable disc – one which holds the system programs – the computer can get itself going by loading them into its memory. It's a bit like the computer pulling itself up by its own bootstraps. Hence the terms, Bootstrapping, Booting, Rebooting, which all refer to the process of supplying the computer with the operating programs it needs.

When you start up your PCW to use LocoScript, you put the LocoScript disc into the A: drive slot. The computer then 'reads-in' the operating system, so everything works properly and then it reads-in LocoScript so you can start work.

But you will know that you don't have to use the LocoScript disc to start the computer. You can also start up by using the disc that is labelled CP/M Plus. Try this:

What CP/M is and why you need it

1 Switch on your system and put your working copy of the disc labelled **CP/M Plus** into the slot of drive A: and make sure it clicks into position. (Remember, it is best not to switch the computer on or off with a disc in the drive.)

After a few moments you will see a pattern of black horizontal lines filling the screen from the top down. Then you will hear the printer resetting itself and you will get CP/M's 'sign-on screen' (see below).

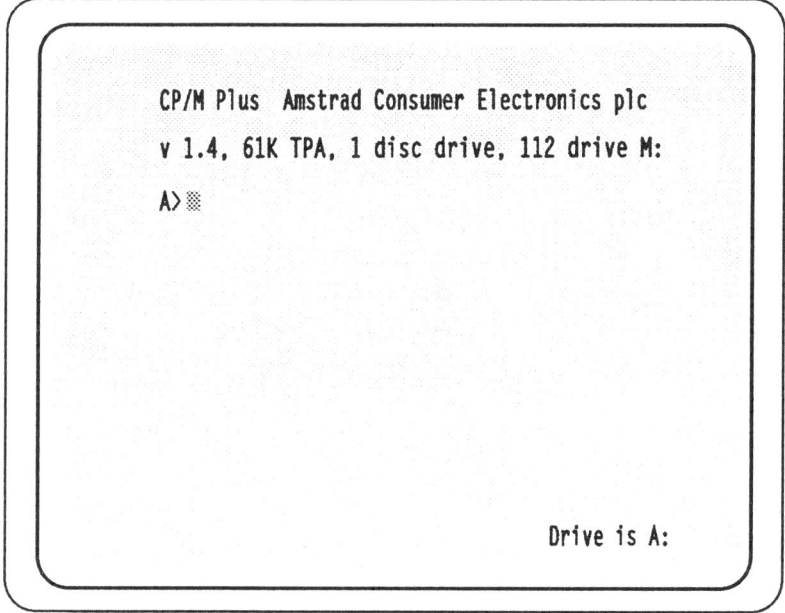

Figure 1-1:   **The CP/M Sign-on Screen. (PCW8256 illustrated)**

What CP/M is and why you need it

2 If the computer does nothing but bleat at you in a plaintive way, make sure that you have the correct side of the disc in drive A: (facing left on the PCW8256 and 8512 and uppermost on a PCW9000 series machine). Make sure the disc is properly home. Then tap the **SPACEBAR** and the PCW should start up.

You are now ready to begin work directly with CP/M Plus. But what does that mean? What work!? And how does having CP/M make that work possible? And how do you get CP/M to do these things? Well, that's what this book is about. These are the very questions which the following pages will try to answer for you. But first, let us take a closer look at CP/M itself.

The basic components of CP/M

It is important to realise that there are really two separate parts to CP/M Plus:

- The operating program which tells the computer how to work and

- A range of sub-programs or routines which enable you to command the computer to do certain jobs for you. In the CP/M jargon these sub-programs are known simply as commands, command programs (or, utilities).

Some of the command sub-programs are built-in to the operating program and are loaded into memory when you start up the computer. They stay in the computer's memory all the time it is switched on. This means that they are available to you any time you are working with CP/M. When you want to use one of these commands, all you have to do is type in its name followed by certain other details (more of which later).

But there is a range of other command programs which are stored on your CP/M discs. These are not loaded into memory when you start up. They include the less frequently used CP/M utility programs as well as enhancements to some of the built-in commands. When you want to use any of this second range of command programs, you will have to put a working copy of one of your CP/M discs into the disc drive so the computer can load the appropriate program into its memory before doing the job you've asked it to do. As these programs do not stay in memory all the time, they have come to be known as transient commands. So remember there are two types of command: permanent and transient.

What jobs can you do with CP/M?

Let's assume you have been using the PCW with LocoScript for some time. For each piece of work you do, LocoScript will create a 'file' and save your work in the relevant file. It is best to think of individual bits of work, and indeed, different computer programs as separate distinct 'files', even though the contents of those files (the records) may be scattered all over the disc. (You don't have to worry about that scattering of records, because the computer sorts it all out for you.)

Eventually, when you try to save another file, you'll get a message telling you that the disc is full. Now, with CP/M you have several ways around this problem. For example:

- You could simply **ERASE** all the files from the disc. But that defeats the whole reason for having discs as a permanent storage medium.

- You could **ERASE** some files on the disc.

- You could **CREATE** a new **DATA DISC**.

- You could **COPY** some files from the disc onto another disc and then **ERASE** the originals to make some space.

- But perhaps what you should have done is **CHECK** how much **FREE SPACE** was left on the disc before you started work!

These are all housekeeping activities – ones which don't contribute directly to your work, but nevertheless they are essential if you are to stay in control of your work.

Housekeeping tasks we shall examine

Here is a list of the things which virtually every PCW user will want to do at some time or other, and which we shall be covering.

- Making the computer do a series of jobs with one command
- Creating certain kinds of useful text files with **RPED**

File management tasks

- Naming files
- Renaming files
- Copying files
- Erasing files

Disc Management tasks

- Formatting discs (preparing them for use)
- Making a system disc (one which 'starts-up' the system)
- Finding out about the files on a disc
- Finding out how much room is left on a disc
- Copying discs (making 'back-ups')

Hardware Adjustments

- Changing the way the keyboard works
- Setting up a modem or another printer

So let's start looking at them, one by one, straight away.

Making the computer do a series of jobs with one command

1 Switch on your system and then put your working copy of the disc labelled **CP/M Plus** into the slot of drive A: and make sure it clicks into position. (Remember, it is best not to switch the computer on or off with a disc in the drive.)

2 If the computer does nothing but bleat its discomfort, make sure that you have the correct side of the disc in drive A:. Make sure the disc is properly home. Then tap the **SPACEBAR** and you should see the screen start displaying a series of black lines as it starts up. You will also hear the printer reset itself.

3 When you get the sign-on screen (see Figure 1-1), key-in (in lower case or in capitals): (a) With an 8000 series machine, **TYPE PROFILE.ENG** – or (b) With a 9000 series machine, **TYPE PROFILE.SUB**. Apart from the case, make sure you copy this exactly. The spacing and the punctuation are very important. If you make a mistake, use the ←DEL key to space back and rub out the error. Then key-in the correction.

You have just keyed-in a CP/M command. This one has two parts, some have less and some have more, but they all have one thing in common. The first word you key-in is the name of one of CP/M's command sub-programs (either built-in or transient).

Making the computer do a series of jobs with one command

'TYPE' is a built-in command. The second part, 'PROFILE.ENG' (or 'PROFILE.SUB') is the name of a file which is on your CP/M disc; the one you have in drive A:. The command you have keyed-in says to the computer, 'Read the contents of a file called PROFILE.ENG (or PROFILE.SUB) on the disc in drive A: and then display them on the screen, so I can read them.' This may not seem very relevant to what we are doing, but bear with me ...

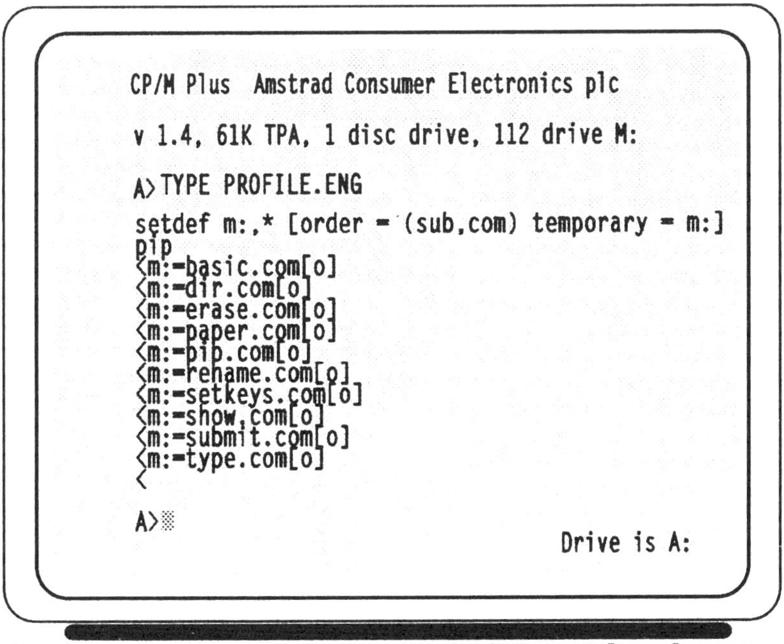

```
CP/M Plus  Amstrad Consumer Electronics plc
v 1.4, 61K TPA, 1 disc drive, 112 drive M:
A>TYPE PROFILE.ENG
setdef m:,* [order = (sub,com) temporary = m:]
pip
<m:=basic.com[o]
<m:=dir.com[o]
<m:=erase.com[o]
<m:=paper.com[o]
<m:=pip.com[o]
<m:=rename.com[o]
<m:=setkeys.com[o]
<m:=show.com[o]
<m:=submit.com[o]
<m:=type.com[o]
<
A>
                                    Drive is A:
```

Figure 1-2:   **Listing the contents of PROFILE.ENG on Screen. (PCW8256)**

PROFILE.ENG or .SUB

Of course, nothing has actually happened yet, so tap the **{RETURN}** key, or the **{ENTER}** key and watch what does happen.

Your screen should end up looking something like the one in Figure 1-2.

'PROFILE.something' is a text file that contains nothing but commands which CP/M can understand. In fact it is an 'ASCII' text file, which means that the letters and symbols in it have been saved in the ASCII format which is readable by pretty well any personal computer. (ASCII stands for 'American Standard Code for Information Interchange')

Note

Text files produced by LocoScript, or most other off-the-shelf word processing programs are saved in a format which is specific to the word processor in question. The text is interspersed with command codes which lay the text out in a particular way on the page. But CP/M and other operating systems cannot usually interpret these codes properly. For example, if you were to command CP/M to 'TYPE' a LocoScript text file, such as the document called 'READ.ME' all you would get on screen is, **'JOYTemplate for Letters group'** and 6 graphics symbols. But if you have read this document while using LocoScript, or if you have printed it out, you will know it is two and a half pages long! What's more, the legend **'JOYTemplate for Letters group'** and the 6 graphics symbols don't appear in the file at all.

PROFILE.ENG or .SUB

Because ASCII files have so many uses, most word processing programs have a facility for creating ASCII files from their own standard format (e.g. in LocoScript it is under the **F7 Modes** option from the Disc Management (Main) screen).

So CP/M can read and understand the commands which are in the 'PROFILE' file. We shall see later on what the various commands mean, but for the moment it is enough to know that each line of the PROFILE text is a separate CP/M command. But why would anyone want to create a text file which contains nothing but CP/M commands? Here again we need to digress a bit.

CP/M has a transient command program called SUBMIT.COM (all CP/M transient command programs have a file name which ends with '.COM' - see Figure 1-2 for a short list). SUBMIT.COM is useful, because it enables you to 'submit' a list of commands by just keying-in one command to get the ball rolling.

The command takes the form **SUBMIT** followed by the name of an ASCII text file which contains the list of commands you want carried out. From what we have seen so far, you might think that all you have to do is key-in a command like **SUBMIT MYASCII.TXT** (assuming you had a file with that name). But, if you were to try it all that would result would be a message on screen which says: **ERROR: No 'SUB' File Found**. That's because the text file you submit for processing must have a file name which ends in .SUB. So, if you have a file called MYASCII.SUB, and it holds CP/M command lines, then the SUBMIT command will work.

Copying a file and giving the copy a different name

It follows that if, on an 8000 series machine, we rename PROFILE.ENG and call it PROFILE.SUB we will end up with a submit file that works.

Note

> If you have a 9512 machine you already have a file called PROFILE.SUB so we shall have to rename that one too.

In fact, we won't simply rename the file, we'll COPY it under a different name, so we don't change the original when we add more commands to the PROFILE.SUB file later in this book.

1 If you have a **PCW8256 or 8512**, key-in this command exactly: **PIP A:PROFILE.SUB=A:PROFILE.ENG[V]**, but don't tap {RETURN} yet.

2 If you have a **PCW9512**, key-in this command exactly: **PIP A:PROFILE.ENG=A:PROFILE.SUB[V]**, but don't tap {RETURN} yet.

3 If you make a mistake use the ←DEL key to rub out the error and then make your correction. Check that your version is exactly the same as the one shown here, and then tap the **{RETURN}** key.

Copying a file and giving the copy a different name

Notes

a. In future I shall refer to the **{RETURN}** key only, even though the **{ENTER}** key will give you the same result (unlike when you are working in LocoScript where the keys do different jobs).

b. 'PIP' is CP/M's copying program (its name stands for 'Peripheral Interchange Program' - 'peripherals' being the various bits of essential hardware which surround the computer, which is at the heart of the system.)

The command we saw on the previous page has a number of features which we shall be covering at the appropriate time in this book, so don't worry about what it all means for the time being. Just be assured that you will end up with two copies of the same file, but under two different names.

One will be called PROFILE.SUB and the other, PROFILE.ENG. In this book we shall be working with PROFILE.SUB, but you will always be able to go back to the original (PROFILE.ENG) if you want to.

Submitting a list of commands

1 When you get the **A>** system prompt back on screen, try keying-in the command **SUBMIT PROFILE** and tapping **{RETURN}**.

You will see the PCW go through a long series of actions, then you will get the **A>** system prompt back. As CP/M carries out each instruction in the list it 'echoes' the instruction on screen. So what are the effects of the PROFILE.SUB commands?

The first command tells the computer where to search for files when it's asked to carry out a command: you will see that it will look first in the M: memory drive, then it will look on the 'default' drive. Most usually that will be drive A:. Also, we have seen that:

- CP/M's command program files have names which end in .COM

- To use a command program all you have to do is key-in the part of the name before the full stop, or dot. (e.g. We used PIP.COM earlier, but the command we actually keyed-in was **PIP** A:PROFILE.SUB=A:PROFILE.ENG[V] not **PIP.COM** etc., etc.).

The first command in the PROFILE.SUB file, (as well as setting the drive search path), assigns these features of .COM files to files with the suffix .SUB. This means that if you want to submit a list of commands, held in a .SUB file, you can now do it much more easily.

Submitting a list of commands

1   Having already submitted the PROFILE.SUB commands file: Key-in the word **PROFILE** and tap **{RETURN}**.

Note

You did not have to type in the full command 'SUBMIT PROFILE' this time. The .SUB file behaved as if it were a .COM program file because of the first command line in the PROFILE.SUB file. This is a very useful feature, as we shall see. This first command has changed the order in which CP/M will look for different types of file. If you had typed in the name of a file – without the dot and a suffix – before you ran PROFILE.SUB, CP/M would have searched for a file with the same name and with the suffix .COM. So, if you keyed in the name FRED and tapped {RETURN}, it would hunt around for a file called FRED.COM. (It's too daft to know there isn't one on the disc). Likewise, if you had keyed in PROFILE and tapped {RETURN} it would have looked for a file called PROFILE.COM. And it would not have found one, so it wouldn't have done anything other than display '**PROFILE?**'.

But now, after running PROFILE.SUB, if you key-in FRED and tap {RETURN}, CP/M will look first for a file called FRED.SUB and when it can't find it, it will look for a file called FRED.COM before it gives up and goes **FRED?**. And, as we have seen, when we key in PROFILE and {RETURN} it, CP/M will execute the list of commands exactly as if PROFILE.SUB were a command file. As you work through this book you'll see that this can save a lot of energy.

27

Submitting a list of commands

The remaining commands in PROFILE.COM are PIP commands. That is, they are copy commands. CP/M will start by calling up the PIP program and then it will copy each of the files in the list, from the disc in drive A: (they are all CP/M transient program files, by the way), and put them one by one into the (M:) memory drive. Then it returns you to the **A>** system prompt.

If you agree with me that it would be much better to call up .SUB files and use them like program files .... and that it would be quite useful to have some of the more commonly used CP/M command programs to hand in the memory drive (especially when CP/M will look in that drive first when you call one up), then it makes sense to implement PROFILE.SUB each time we start up under CP/M. Better still if we could get CP/M to implement it automatically.

In fact we can. When you boot the system, the PCW loads in the CP/M operating program and then it looks for a file called PROFILE.SUB and runs through the commands in the file with that name. (if the file is called something else, such as PROFILE.ENG for example, then it cannot run through the commands). But if there is a file called PROFILE.SUB on the disc in drive A:, then it is implemented automatically. (It makes you wonder why the file was called PROFILE.ENG on the 8000 series. Perhaps Amstrad weren't convinced of its usefulness in the early PCW days.)

Let's prove, that by re-booting or re-setting the system, we run PROFILE.SUB automatically. Remember, the disc does now have a file called PROFILE.SUB.

Submitting PROFILE.SUB automatically on start-up

1 Hold down the left hand **SHIFT** key and the **EXTRA** key together, then tap the **EXIT** key. Release all the keys and watch the screen.

When you re-set, or re-boot, or start-up in the morning with a disc which contains a file called PROFILE.SUB, the PCW will go through its normal booting routine – displaying the black lines and resetting the printer – and then it will execute the commands in PROFILE.SUB before it displays the **A>** system prompt.

Now, each time you start up or re-set with the disc you have in drive A: at the moment, your PCW will be set up as we have been discussing in the last few pages.

If for some reason you don't want that to happen, then work through the action paragraph on the next page, though please read the note below, before you do.

Note

I strongly advise you to leave things as they are while you are working through this book, because it assumes that the PCW has been set up with PROFILE.SUB and we shall be adding to the list of commands in the file later on. To leave things as they are now – particularly if you have a PCW9512 – skip the action paragraph on the next page.

Erasing PROFILE.SUB

1 To get rid of the file called PROFILE.SUB **(but, see the note at the end of the previous page, first)**, key-in: **ERA** (short for 'erase'), a space and then **PROFILE.SUB**.
i.e.   **ERA PROFILE.SUB** and tap **{RETURN}**.

Now when you start up the PCW will not be able to implement the commands in the PROFILE file. But you still have your copy of PROFILE.ENG which you can use to re-create a different PROFILE.SUB file if you want to at some later stage.

So far we have been concentrating on PROFILE.SUB, but only as an example of what .SUB files can do. But you can create your own .SUB files to do the jobs you want to do. So, how do we create a new .SUB file?

It is actually very simple. All you have to do is create an ASCII text file which contains a list of CP/M commands. And you can do that by using LocoScript in the normal way and then converting the finished file into ASCII format (through the **F7 Modes** menu from the Disc Management screen). But a much easier and quicker way is to use RPED, a simple text editing programme which is supplied on your CP/M disc. RPED is not one of the normal set of CP/M programs. It is an extra supplied with the PCW.

The text editor supplied with CP/M is called ED.COM. I find it excessively cumbersome to use, so I shall not be recommending it at all in this book. But we should have a look at RPED.

Using the RPED text editor

1 Start up your PCW in the normal way under CP/M (using the start-up disc which has our copy of PROFILE.SUB on it).

2 When you get the **A>** system prompt, key-in **RPED** and tap **{RETURN}**.

The PCW will load the 'BASIC' programming language, which will then run RPED. After a few moments your screen will sort itself out and you will get RPED's opening screen, which looks like this:

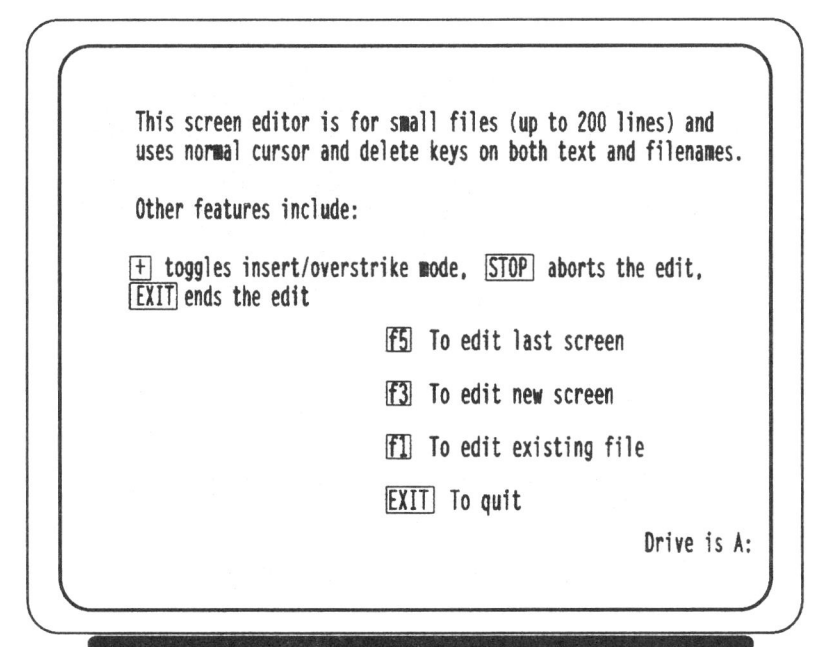

```
This screen editor is for small files (up to 200 lines) and
uses normal cursor and delete keys on both text and filenames.

Other features include:

[+] toggles insert/overstrike mode, [STOP] aborts the edit,
[EXIT] ends the edit
                    [f5] To edit last screen
                    [f3] To edit new screen
                    [f1] To edit existing file
                    [EXIT] To quit
                                              Drive is A:
```

Figure 1-3: **The RPED opening screen**

31

Using the RPED text editor

The RPED opening screen uses reverse video in several places to highlight certain key points, which is fine on the computer screen, but it does not transpose to paper very well, as you can see in Figure 1-3. So let me take a few moments to translate what it says. At the top it explains that RPED is a 'screen editor' designed to help you create and edit 'small' files of up to 200 lines of text. Reading between the lines (Ho, ho!), I would guess that it was originally developed to help people write computer programs conveniently.

When you create a file with RPED, the keyboard cursor control arrows, the other cursor movement keys (such as 'LINE', 'EOL' and '{RETURN}') as well as the delete keys, all work as they do under LocoScript. When you start keying-in text RPED is set up to allow you to insert characters into existing text. You simply move the cursor to where you want to insert a character or some words and then key-in the new text. This is because 'insert mode' is switched on automatically when you start up. (But keep an eye on the length of your lines of text when you insert text into an existing line.)

There may be times, though when you want to overtype and replace a letter or some words rather than insert new ones. So, to switch insert mode OFF, you tap the **[+] SET** key, to the left of the **SPACEBAR**. (Not to be confused with + plus key which is at the top of the keyboard; i.e. the = 'equals' key shifted.) To switch insert mode back on again, just tap **[+] SET** once more. So, in the jargon, the [+] SET key is a 'toggle switch' which 'toggles between insert mode and overtype mode'.

Using the RPED text editor

If you want to stop the edit and abandon the work you have done, simply tap the **STOP** key (top left corner of the keyboard), or you can hold down the **ALT** key and at the same time tap the letter **C**, then release both keys.

Note

This combination, **ALT-C**, is one of many codes which CP/M understands (we shall look at some more of them later when we are examining the workings of the keyboard in more detail). Such combinations are known as 'ALT Codes', or more usually when you are dealing with CP/M, as 'Control Codes'. (In this book I shall use both terms.)

So, if at some time in the future, you see a reference to **ALT-C**, or **CONTROL-C**, or **Ctrl-C**, or even just **^C**, then, for the PCW, read it as: 'Hold down ALT and tap the letter C'.

When you have finished creating your text and checked that it is correct, you tap the **EXIT** key to finish and to save your work.

Those are the basic things you need to know about using RPED, so let us look at how to create and edit files.

33

RPED - creating a new file

1 With RPED's opening screen displayed, tap the **f3/f4** key.

RPED asks you to give it a name for the file you are about to create.

Note

RPED forces you to prefix the file name with 'a:' (which is the same as A: to the PCW), the name of your start-up disc drive. This means that when you come to save the file at the end of the editing session, your work will be saved on the disc in drive A:. If you are using a PCW8000 series machine and you have an exact copy of your CP/M master disc in drive A:, there will be only about 3k of space left on the disc. While that may be enough for the short file we are about to create, it is getting very close to the limit. In any case, it is always a good idea to keep your work separate from programs, so, put another (data) disc in drive A: before you go any further. If you do not have another data disc available and you do not know how to create one, see the section in this book titled, appropriately enough, 'Creating a data disc'.

RPED will enable us to create an ASCII text file which we can use for a number of different purposes. But for this exercise we shall simply create a .SUB file to continue our theme of getting the computer to do several jobs with a single command. So:

2 Key-in (in upper or lower case), the file name **FILES.SUB** and tap the **{RETURN}** key.

RPED - creating a new file

After a short pause, the opening screen clears and you get RPED's editing screen. The information along the top line is probably self-explanatory, but there are a couple of new ideas we need to look at. First, let us assume you have created a few lines of text and you suddenly realise that you have left out one of the commands you meant to put in.

Each command in a .SUB file has to appear on a separate line, so you will have to create a new line for the command you want to insert. Working in LocoScript you would probably move the cursor to the start of the line which is where you want the new line to be, then you would key-in the relevant text and simply tap {RETURN} at the end to move the original text down a line. But that won't work with RPED. Instead, you have to move the cursor to the line which is currently where you want the new line to be, hold down the **ALT** key and then tap the ↓ **ARROW** key to move the existing line (and all the ones that follow it) down one line. If you want to create two blank lines, simply tap **ALT-**↓ **ARROW** again.

The second new idea comes about if, after checking the text you have keyed-in, you decide that one of the command lines is redundant. Simply move the cursor to the line in question (anywhere on the line) and tap the **CUT** key. The line in question will disappear and all the other text will move up a line to close the gap.

With the exception of those two points, using RPED to create a text file – whether it be a .SUB file or a computer program written in the BASIC programming language – is very straightforward

RPED - creating a new file

3 With RPED's cursor in the top left of the work area, key-in: **DIR A:** and tap **{RETURN}** to move the cursor down to the next line. Then key-in: **DIR M:** and tap **{RETURN}**.

Note

The 'DIR' command is covered in much more detail in the next chapter. For our purposes here it is enough to know that DIR causes CP/M to give you a list of the files on (or a DIRectory of) the disc which is in the drive you specify in the command (A: in the first line and M: in the second). But, if you do not specify a drive name in the command line CP/M will assume that you want a directory of the disc you are working on at the time.

The two lines we have keyed-in are very short, but if you want to key-in a very long line of text you might run into a problem with RPED. Unlike LocoScript and other word processing programs, RPED does not move your cursor down and to the left when it reaches the right hand side of the 'screen page'. So you have to keep an eye on the cursor and be ready to tap {RETURN} when it gets too close to the right 'margin', though this is unlikely to happen when you are keying-in a command line. Remember also that for CP/M, command lines have to be on a single line of their own.

4 Tap **EXIT** to save our work and, when you get RPED's opening screen back, tap **EXIT** again to close down RPED.

RPED- editing an existing file

1 Let us try out our .SUB file to see what it does. Key in the word **FILES** and tap **{RETURN}**.

CP/M will run the file called FILES.SUB and carry out the two commands. It will read the disc in drive A: and display a list of the files on it, then it will read the M: (memory) drive and list the files on there.

I think that display looks a bit cluttered – the two file lists are too close together – so let's improve the display a little by making the computer skip a couple of lines between the two file lists. We do that by amending, or editing, our FILES.SUB file with RPED.

1 If you have saved **FILES.SUB** on a data disc (not on your copy of the CP/M disc), then you will need to start by **putting the copy of the CP/M disc in drive A:**.

2 Key-in **RPED** and tap **{RETURN}**. When you get RPED's opening screen: **If you saved FILES.SUB on a separate data disc, put the data disc in drive A: and tap the f1/f2 key.** Otherwise, just tap the **f1/f2** key to edit an existing file on the CP/M disc.

3 When RPED asks you for the file name, key-in **FILES.SUB** and tap **{RETURN}**. When RPED asks you to confirm the name and destination for the amended file, (see Figure 1-4) just tap **{RETURN}** again to get the text you keyed in earlier onto the screen.

37

RPED- editing an existing file

4 Move the cursor down to the second line by tapping the ↓ ARROW. Then hold down the **ALT** key and tap ↓ ARROW twice to create two blank lines. Release the **ALT** key and tap the **EXIT** key twice: once to save the amended file and once to close down RPED.

Now let us see what happens when we run the FILES.SUB commands.

1 Key-in **FILES** and tap {RETURN}.

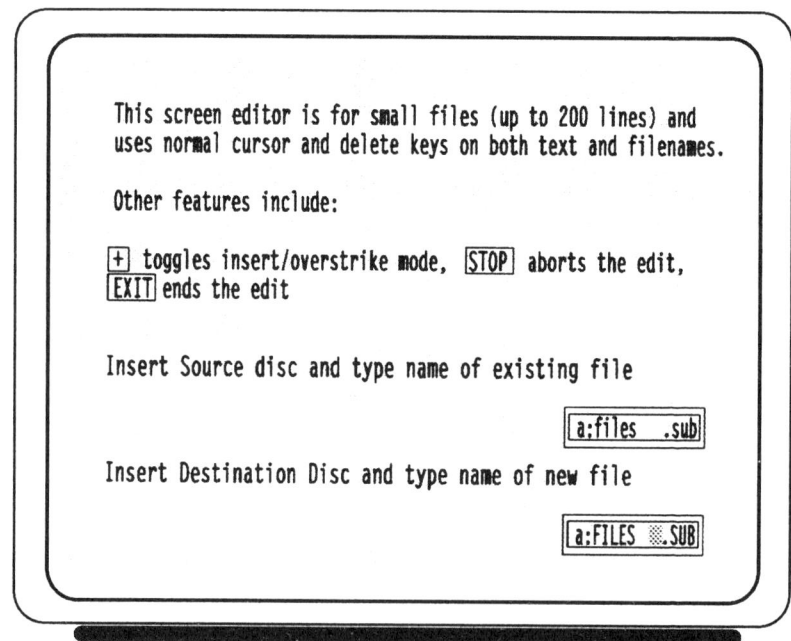

```
This screen editor is for small files (up to 200 lines) and
uses normal cursor and delete keys on both text and filenames.

Other features include:

[+] toggles insert/overstrike mode, [STOP] aborts the edit,
[EXIT] ends the edit

Insert Source disc and type name of existing file
                                              [a:files   .sub]
Insert Destination Disc and type name of new file
                                              [a:FILES  .SUB]
```

Figure 1-4: **RPED opening screen - editing an existing file**

RPED- editing an existing file

This time, I think you'll agree the display of file names has a better layout, it looks less cluttered then it did.

So we have seen how to use RPED to create a SUBMIT file – in fact, any ASCII text file – and we have seen how useful .SUB files can be. If, after reading this book, you develop particular housekeeping routines which you carry out regularly, give serious thought to producing a SUBMIT file to make your job easier.

We shall be coming back to SUBMIT files later in this book when we add a few more useful tweaks to the PROFILE.SUB file.

Chapter 2
Managing Files

Naming and storing files

When you create a document file (or any other kind of file) which you intend to store on a disc, you will have to give it a name. That name will have to conform with the following simple rules:

- Two parts: The file names you use can have two parts: a **TITLE** and a code to identify what type of file it is (e.g. whether it is a command program, a submit file, a letter, a quotation, etc.)

- You don't have to use both parts, but if you do, you must separate them with a full-stop (or 'dot'), e.g. 'PROFILE.SUB'

- The **TITLE** can be between 1 and 8 characters in length

- The **TYPE** code can be between 1 and 3 characters in length

- You must not have a space anywhere in your file name and you must not use a full stop other than to separate the title and the type code. If you need to split the file title into more than one part (e.g. chapters of a book), use the underscore symbol, e.g. 'CPM_BK_1.TXT'

You can use most of the keys on the keyboard in your file names, but for day to day purposes I would advise you to stick to letters and numbers. You won't make any mistakes that way, but perhaps more importantly, you're more likely to be able to interpret your file names in six months time. After all, you store a file so you can refer to it at some time in the future and that means you must be able to find the file again. So keep your file names simple! Use a system that comes naturally to you, or one that fits in with the way you do things normally.

Naming and storing files

It doesn't matter whether you key-in the file name in capitals or in lower case. The computer will convert all letters into capitals.

Note

Certain file TYPE codes have specific meanings to your computer, and some have specific meanings to particular software packages, so be careful with them. In particular do not use: '.COM' '.EXE' '.HEX' '.ASM' '.BAS' '.PRN' '.INT' '.SUB' '.$$$' unless you know what they represent and you intend to create a particular kind of file which normally has the suffix you will be using.

Matching up file names ('masks')

Quite often you will want to carry out the same command for several files with very similar names (for example, make a copy of a set of files called 'chap1, chap2, chap3, etc.'. Or perhaps to look for a file whose name you cannot remember exactly). For times like this CP/M allows you to use 'ambiguous file names' in many of the commands.

You create an ambiguous file name by replacing parts of the name with special symbols. You can use the question mark symbol (?) to represent a single character or you can use the asterisk (*) symbol to represent a group of characters. e.g.

1 To make a copy on drive M: of several files, all called 'chap followed by a number, (which are on the disc in drive A:) you would key-in: **PIP M:=A:CHAP? {RETURN}**
In response to this single command, CP/M will copy all the files which match the ambiguous name.

2 To find a file called 'LETTER.(something-or-other)', key-in:
DIR LETTER.* {RETURN}

In the first example you could have used **CHAP*** as your ambiguous filename. In the second example you could have used **LETTER.???** Just remember that a question mark takes the place of a single character and the asterisk represents several characters. So **????????.???** and ***.*** both mean 'all files called something dot something'. In other words, all files!

45

Matching up file names ('masks')

- So the command: DIR followed by either of these two and then {RETURN} will give you a normal directory:
  e.g. **DIR *.* {RETURN}**

- **????????** or ***** on its own means all files which do not have a file TYPE extension.
  e.g. **DIR ???????? {RETURN}**

- **????.*** means any file which has only four characters in the first name and has any file type extension.

- ***.?** means a file which has any name, but which has only one character in its file type extension. There are lots more possible combinations for you to try.

Renaming a file

From time to time you will want to give your files different names. For example, because you have changed your filing system, or more often because you want to denote that a file is a 'back-up' copy of another file.

1   To rename a file which is called LETTER.TXT and to give it the new name LETTER.BAK you would key-in:
   REN LETTER.BAK=LETTER.TXT {RETURN}.

Note

Notice the formula, newname = oldname!

2   If you want to change the name of a file which is on a disc other than the one you are working on (i.e. other than the one you are 'logged to') you will have to precede the file names with the appropriate drive identifying letter. For example, if you are logged to drive M: and you want to change the name of a file which is on drive A: you would key-in:
   REN A:LETTER.BAK=A:LETTER.TXT {RETURN}.

3   If you are logged to drive A: and you want to rename several files on the disc in drive A: which have similar names (e.g. renaming all files called something.LET, changing the names to something.OLD) you can use wild-card characters (or file masks). You would key-in:
   REN *.OLD=*.LET {RETURN}.

Renaming a file

Notes

a. You do not need to put the drive identifier before the file name if you are changing the name of a file which is on the drive you are logged to. (See action paragraph 3 on the previous page.)

b. If you try to change the name of a file to a filename which already exists, a message will appear warning you that there is already a file of that name. You then have the option Y/N to cancel or proceed.

c. The **REName** command changes only the name of the file - it does not affect the file in any other way.

Making a duplicate copy of a file

When you want to tidy-up or reorganise your disc filing system, one of the jobs you will want to do is to make copies of one or more files. Don't forget that you will need to make safety (back-up) copies of all your files in any case.

So how do you make copies of a file rather than a disc? Well you need the CP/M program called **PIP.COM** which is in your memory drive, assuming you started up with a CP/M disc which had PROFILE.SUB on it (see Chapter 1, 'Making the computer do a series of jobs with one command'). You will need your CP/M disc, so make sure you have your working copy of it to hand.

1   Put your working copy of the CP/M disc in drive A:.

2   At the system prompt **A>**, key-in: **M:{RETURN}** You will see the 'system prompt' change to **M>** which tells you that M: is now the active drive.

You have now 'logged' to the M: drive, and consequently it is now what is known as the default drive. Until you logged to M:, drive A: was the active or default drive. The default drive is the one CP/M will work with in default of any instructions to the contrary from you. For example, if you key-in: **DIR {RETURN}** you will get a list of the files on the M: drive rather than the ones on the A: drive.

Making a duplicate copy of a file

3 Leave your CP/M disc in drive A: for the time being. (Remember, that we are 'logged' to the M: drive and there is a copy of PIP.COM on this drive.) Let us suppose you want to make a duplicate copy of a file on the disc in A: which is called 'SHOW.COM' and you want that copy on M:. Key in: **PIP M:SHOW.COM=A:SHOW.COM** (don't press {RETURN} yet).

Notes

a. Remember, you want to use PIP.COM, so that is the first thing you key-in, but, because it is a **COM**mand program you don't need to key-in the full name to run the program.

b. Notice also that the PIP command is separated from the rest of the instruction by a space and that there are no other spaces in the instruction. PIP is the command, the other details are known as the 'parameters' of the command. (There is already a copy of SHOW.COM on drive M:, but it will be overwritten during the copying process.) Also notice how the parameters are expressed. They are in the form of a mathematical equation which describes how you want things to be - rather than what you want PIP to do!

4 Tap **{RETURN}** now to implement the PIP command and thereby make a duplicate copy of the original file.

The TYPE command

In Chapter 1 you used TYPE to list the contents of an ASCII file. At that time, you used the straightforward version of the command, so here I want to expand a little on how else you might want to use it.

When you used the TYPE command before, it was to read the contents of quite a short file. On that occasion the contents of the whole file came up on screen and that was that. But had that file been a long one, TYPE would have displayed the first 28 lines only and then paused to allow you time to read the 'page' on screen. When you were ready to read on you would have had to tap the {RETURN} key (in fact, any key) to bring the next page on screen.

You may remember that if you want to print the contents of the file called, for example, PROFILE.SUB, you go through a procedure like this:

1   Key-in: **TYPE PROFILE.SUB**, but don't press {RETURN} yet. Instead, hold down the **ALT** key and tap the letter **P** to open up the channel to the printer.

2   Check that the printer has paper in it, and that it is on-line and ready to print, then tap the **{RETURN}** key.

The contents of the file will appear on screen and, at the same time, be printed out for you.

3   Remember to tap **ALT-P** to close the printer channel.

TYPE command - enhancements

The procedure on the previous page assumed that the file you wanted to TYPE was on the same disc as the command program TYPE.COM (e.g. on the CP/M disc), or that you have booted-up with PROFILE.SUB on the 8000 series machines. But there will often be times when you want to print out a file which is on a disc which does not contain the command program. Fear not! This is how you do it.

1   **Single drive:** Put, say, your working copy of the CP/M disc in drive A: and key-in **TYPE{RETURN}**. The type command will run and prompt you to enter a file name.

2   Remove the CP/M disc from drive A: and replace it with the disc that contains the file you want to list-out. Key-in the file name, e.g. **MYFILE.ASC** and tap **{RETURN}**.

A general note about commands

All the CP/M commands we examine in this chapter work like this. If you just key-in the command name and tap {RETURN} you will be prompted to supply the rest of the command line. This is a practical measure which avoids the need to have copies of all the command programs on all the discs (and if you decide not to use PROFILE.SUB on your boot disc).

This way you can call up the command program from the disc which holds them and then work on another disc in the same drive.

TYPE command - enhancements

In effect the TYPE command you have seen so far, works as if you had keyed in a command which reads: 'TYPE the contents of the file MYFILE.ASC one screen page at a time and pause at the end of each page.' There will be times when you do not want TYPE to pause at the end of a page – if you are printing it out, for example.

In such cases you use a slightly modified version of the TYPE command. You would:

1   Key-in: **TYPE MYFILE.ASC [NO PAGE] ALT-P {RETURN}**. Or, if the file you want to list-out is on another disc, you would key-in: **TYPE {RETURN}**, change the disc, then **MYFILE.ASC [NO PAGE] ALT-P {RETURN}**. Then tap **ALT-P** again to switch off the printer channel.

The output will go to the screen and to the printer, so you will end up with a clean 'hard-copy' of the contents of the file. These commands will produce a complete and uninterrupted listing of the contents of the file in question. But you can stop TYPE displaying the file contents at any time you want by tapping ALT-S to 'suspend' the listing. Like this:

2   Tap the **COPY** key to repeat the last command you keyed-in (minus the ALT-P), Tap **{RETURN}** and then immediately tap **ALT-S** to stop the display. Then, when you're ready, tap **ALT-Q** to carry on.

Using PIP – enhancements

The basic PIP command is quite easy to use, but there are a lot of refinements to it which you may find useful. Here are the most useful ones. (Incidentally, you will have seen some of them in earlier sections of this book, but this time I'll provide an explanation of what's going on!)

Copy several files with the similar names using the two wild-card characters

E.g. If you want to copy all the 'Submit' files from the disc in drive A: and put them on the memory drive (M:), you would key-in: **PIP M:*.SUB=A:*.SUB** or **PIP M:=A:*.SUB**. If you are logged to A: when you give the command, you can shorten it even further to: **PIP M:=*.SUB**. Because you are logged to A: (i.e. A: is the default drive), PIP will look on the disc in A: for the original file.

Copy an ASCII file to the screen (console) or the printer (list device)

We saw in the first chapter and earlier in this one that you can get CP/M to list the contents of a file on screen by using the 'TYPE' command. You can achieve the same end with PIP by replacing the destination file name with a destination 'Device Name'. You have already seen several examples of the principle of device names when I have referred to 'drive A:' or 'drive M:'. The A: and the M: are disc drive names.

Using PIP – enhancements

Your computer system has various parts, the keyboard, the printer, the screen, the drives, etc. and each one of these has to have a label of some kind (a device name) so you can direct information to specific places (devices) in the system. So, if you want to direct the contents of a file on the disc in drive A: called PROFILE.SUB to the screen, or console – which has the device name CON: (with the colon at the end being an integral part of the name) then you would key-in:
PIP CON:=A:PROFILE.SUB and then tap **{RETURN}**.
Try it and see what happens, but put your CP/M disc in drive A: first.

Similarly you can copy the file PROFILE.SUB direct to the printer in two ways. If you want to do it with TYPE, this is what you key-in: Start by tapping **ALT-P** key combination (**CONTROL-P**, or **^P** if you prefer. They all mean the same thing; 'hold down the ALT key and tap the letter P'). This opens up a channel between the screen and the printer so it will echo everything that appears on the screen. Now put some paper in the printer (don't forget to exit from Printer Control Mode after you've done it), then key-in: **TYPE A:PROFILE.SUB** and tap **{RETURN}**. When the printer stops, tap **ALT-P** again to close the printer channel

When you copy a file to the printer (device name LST:), using PIP, you don't need to key-in ALT-P first. The PIP command itself opens up the channel and closes it again when it has finished. So to achieve nearly the same end result as in the previous paragraph, key-in: **PIP LST:=A:PROFILE.SUB** and tap **{RETURN}**. The slight difference with PIP is the contents of the file are not repeated on screen.

55

Using PIP – enhancements

Sending information from the keyboard directly to the printer

I'm not sure how useful this trick will be to you, but I include it just in case. Make sure you have some paper in the printer and it is on-line and ready to go. Then key-in: **PIP LST:=CON:** and tap {RETURN}. Nothing much will seem to happen, apart from the printer making a noise. But notice that the system prompt is no longer on screen. Tap **ALT-J** a couple of times and listen to the printer. You will hear it, and perhaps see it, execute a couple line feeds. Now this tells you two things: Firstly the keyboard has an open channel to the printer and secondly that ALT-J (^J) is the control code which generates a line feed for you. Now key-in, **THE QUICK RED FOX**, but nothing else. No typing has appeared on the printer yet, but now tap **^J** again. You will hear the printer printing the words you keyed-in.

But if you look at the screen you will see that the cursor has moved down a line, but it has not moved back to the left. Tap **^M** and you'll see it jump to the left. So when we key-in a bit of text we need to tap ^J then ^M before we type the next line. Now key-in, **JUMPS OVER THE LAZY BROWN DOG ^J^M**.

So that's how it works, but how do you get out of it? Simple, Tap **^Z** which is the control code that means 'end of file' and you will get the system prompt back. So, remember, ^J is the code for a line feed, ^M is a carriage return and ^Z means end of file.

Using PIP – enhancements

Sending information from the keyboard and creating a new file on disc

If you want to create a very short ASCII file, like FILES.SUB we created earlier, this method is even quicker than using RPED. The only disadvantage is that you cannot edit the file while you are creating it. Even so, let's produce another version of FILES.SUB under a different name. Let's call it DRIVES.SUB and let's create it on the M: drive.

Key in: **PIP M:DRIVES.SUB=CON:** and tap **{RETURN}**. Now **very carefully** key-in,

>	**DIR A:** followed by **ALT-J ALT-M**
>	**DIR M:** followed by **ALT-J ALT-M**
>	**ALT-Z**

We can now see if our new .SUB file works. Key-in **DRIVES** and tap **{RETURN}**.

As you can see this is quite a useful way to create a very short ASCII file, but you do have to be very careful when you key things in, because none of the editing keys seem to work in PIP on the PCW. If you do make a mistake, let's say you keyed in 'DOR A:' by mistake, then the best thing to do is to tap ^Z, erase the file you have just created and start again.

57

Using PIP – enhancements

Copying several files into one big one

Let us say, for example, that you want to tack the commands in your FILES.SUB file onto the end of the list of commands in PROFILE.SUB. We shall create a single file which holds all the commands and we shall save it on drive M: under the name BIGFILE.SUB. I shall start with the assumption that you have the source files, but on separate discs (one on the CP/M start-up disc and one on a data disc). So we need to look at another way of using PIP.COM. At the same time we shall look at another useful refinement on the way we use PIP.

1   Key in: **PIP** and tap **{RETURN}**.

PIP will run and it will display an asterisk as prompt. It is saying, 'I'm ready to copy things, what do you want to do?' First, we shall copy our source files onto the M: drive.

2   With your CP/M start-up disc in A:, key-in: **M:=A:*.SUB[C] {RETURN}**. (You do not have begin the command by typing PIP again, because PIP is already running.)

Note

The '[C]' at the end of the command tells PIP to check, or confirm, that you do want to copy the file it names. If you do want to copy it, you tap the letter **Y**, if not you tap the letter **N**.

Using PIP – enhancements

3   PIP should be displaying the name of the first .SUB file it has found, followed by '(Y/N)'. Let us say, for the sake of this example, it has found RPED.SUB. You don't want to copy this one, so tap the letter **N**. PIP will then move on to find another .SUB file and it will display its name followed by '(Y/N)' again. If PIP is displaying the name of one of the files you want, tap **Y**.

PIP will continue to search for .SUB files, so if it displays any names, other than the names of the files you want, tap **N**. When it can find no more .SUB files, it stops searching and displays the asterisk prompt to tell you it has finished the job you asked it to do.

4   Now put your data disc in drive A:.

Here is a handy general tip that will come in useful time and time again. We have a situation now where you need to repeat the last procedure you carried out – in this instance you need to copy one .SUB file from the disc in A: and put it on the M: drive. This means you need the same command as before, but, if you are as lazy as me, you won't want to key it in all over again ... and you needn't.

5   Instead, tap the **COPY** key and let CP/M type out the last command you gave it. Then tap **{RETURN}** to implement the command. As before, Copy only the file that you want. Tap **N** if PIP displays any other .SUB file names.

Using PIP – enhancements

Note

Incidentally, if you want to give CP/M or PIP nearly the same command as last time, you can tap the COPY key to re-type the last command and then edit the command with the normal editing keys before you tap {RETURN}.

6 With both our source files on drive M: and PIP is still running, key-in: **M:BIGFILE.SUB=M:PROFILE.SUB,M:FILES.SUB {RETURN}.**

Notice how we have to include the location of the various files in the file name (e.g. M:BIGFILE.SUB). This is because we are still logged to drive A: and we want to create the new file on drive M:, from source files which are also on drive M:. One way to avoid having to key-in the M: all the time would be to log to drive M: before keying-in the command, but you would only have to log back drive A: before doing what we are going to do next, so it makes little real difference.

7 To check the contents of our new .SUB file, tap **{RETURN}** to finish working with PIP and then key-in: **TYPE M:BIGFILE.SUB** and **{RETURN}** it. You will see that our new file contains the text of both source files. To check that the new .SUB file works, key-in: **M:BIGFILE {RETURN}** and watch the screen. If you have your data disk in drive A: you will get various error messages, but that doesn't matter now. The important thing to notice is that the file is attempting to do what you want.

Using PIP – enhancements

We just saw that if you include '[C]' at the end of the PIP command line, the PIP program will ask you for confirmation before it copies a file. The [C] is just one of PIP's options and there are several more you can use. If you look on page 79 of the CP/M section of your PCW8000 series User Guide – page 471 of the PCW9512 User Guide – you will find a complete list of these options along with a short description of what they do.

PIP is a program which you can put to very good use, so it is worth spending some time on experimenting with it. So why not give it a try on your own with a disc that holds some old files.

Getting rid of unwanted files

From time to time you will want to clear old files from your discs - to make more room, or simply to minimise the clutter. Here's how you do it.

1 Start by double checking that you really do not need to keep the file. If you do need the file, but you don't want it on the disc you are using, you can copy the file onto another disc.

The structure of the command to use is: ERA followed by the name of the file you want to get rid of, followed by {RETURN}. So, for example, to erase a file called LETTER.TXT which is on the drive you are 'logged' to, you would key-in: **ERA LETTER.TXT, {RETURN}**.

To erase a file which is on a drive other than the one you are logged to, you must precede the file-name with the appropriate drive identifier. e.g. **ERA B:LETTER.TXT {RETURN}**.

To erase a group of files with similar names you can use file name masks, see the section, 'Matching up file names ('masks')'. E.g. You could key-in something like: **ERA B:LETTER.* {RETURN}**. The PCW will check you really do want to erase a number of files. You will have to confirm by tapping the letter **Y**. Now this means you can erase several, or even all, the files on a disc in one go by using file name masks, but be careful – particularly late at night when you are tidying up after a long working session! ERA *.BAK is different from ERA *.* by only two key-strokes, but the end results are totally unalike; the first erases all the .BAK files, the second gets rid of everything. Yet in my experience, this is a very easy mistake to make!

Getting rid of unwanted files

As an added safety measure you can get the PCW to check with you before it erases each file (provided you have a copy of ERASE.COM available preferably on the disc you are logged to).

1 So, assuming you were logged to drive M: with ERASE.COM on the same drive (i.e. copied across from the CP/M disc), you can selectively erase all the files on the disc in drive A: with the command: **ERA A:*.* [C]** then **{RETURN}**.

The PCW will present you with the name of a file on the disc and then ask you to confirm that you do want it erased, before removing the file from the disc.

Note:

The ERAse command does not put the file into 'limbo' as LocoScript's erase/delete procedure does. Once you have ERAsed a file you cannot get it back - unless you have special software.

Protecting files - read only

Judging by the previous section, perhaps the person we most need to protect our files from is ourself. So the system lets us protect our files from a tired person whose mind is in neutral and whose fingers are in fifth gear. Please note, though, that the PCW User Guide advises against protecting files or discs used by LocoScript.

We have already seen that we should make working copies of our software to protect master discs from damage, and we should make back-up copies of our work wherever possible. Some files are vital to the computer, system files, and we can separate these from our document files. Two additional features available to us are, creating Read Only files and adding Password Access to discs and files.

1 Start by getting your working copy of the disc labelled 'CP/M Plus' and put it in drive A:.

2 At the **A>** prompt, key-in **SET PROFILE.SUB[RO]** and tap **{RETURN}**.

Note

RO stands for Read Only, i.e. anyone can examine the file but not edit or erase it. When you create a file for the first time it is an [RW] file, one which can be 'Read' and erased or amended (or 'Written' to). To return an [RO] file to normal, key-in: e.g. **SET PROFILE.SUB [RW] {RETURN}**.

Protecting files
- system files

You can use wild-cards to protect groups of files, as for example if you wanted to make all your 'System' files read only.

Note

'System Files' are ones which are hidden when you list the files on a disc with the normal DIRectory command. They are not copied, erased or renamed along with 'non-system' files.

To separate system files from other files you will first need to label them as system files. So, for example, to set all the .COM files as system files (on your copy of the CP/M start-up disc):

1 With your copy CP/M disc in drive A:, key-in:
SET *.COM [SYS] {RETURN}. The SET command lists each file as it sets it, but notice that, even though they are system files, they are still Read Write files.

If you key-in **DIR {RETURN}** now, you will see that you get a much shorter list of files and the PCW tells you that 'SYSTEM FILE(S) EXIST'.

Note

You will also see a file called 'J14CPM3.EMS'. This file is the one which holds the operating program the PCW needs before it can act as an integrated system. We shall see the significance of this soon.

Protecting files - system files

2   Now, to set all the system files to Read Only, key-in: **SET *.COM [RO] {RETURN}**.

Just to prove to you that system files are not treated like normal files (known as NON-SYSTEM files), we shall copy all the files on the disc in drive A: into the memory drive. So we shall have to start by making room for them in the M: drive.

1   Key-in: **ERA M:*.*** **{RETURN}** and then tap the letter **Y** to confirm that you do want to do this foolish thing.

2   Now key-in **PIP M:=*.*** (remember this command says 'copy all the files on A: onto M:'), and tap **{RETURN}**. Notice that no .COM files are copied across, even though you instructed PIP to copy all the files.

This means that the next time you boot your system with your copy CP/M disc, PIP will not be able to copy the utility files onto drive M:, which makes the PROFILE.SUB file a bit useless. So, we had better return the .COM files to their previous status.

3   Key-in: **SET *.COM [DIR] {RETURN}** and watch the messages on screen. Now reset the PCW by holding down **SHIFT** and **EXTRA** and then tapping **EXIT**. Watch the screen to check that PROFILE.SUB works as it should.

Protecting files - user numbers

With CP/M you can create files which have different User Numbers. In practical terms this might be of interest to you if more than one person uses the PCW. The idea is you can assign a different user number to each person and they log-on to the system with that number. (User numbers can be anything between 0 and 15, but be careful with the numbers 8 to 15 because they might confuse LocoScript.)

For example let's say that your system is used by yourself and two other people (Romeo and Juliet) and that you want to keep your files separate. We'll say that you are user number 0 (zero) and the others are 1 and 2 respectively.

When you start work you do not have to log-on with a user number, because the PCW will start-up automatically under user number 0. When Romeo starts work he would begin by keying-in **USER 1 {RETURN}** and Juliet would begin work by keying-in **USER 2 {RETURN}**.

CP/M responds by displaying a modified system prompt: For Romeo it would be **1A>** and for Juliet it would be **2A>**.

Any files they create while they are logged on with this number will have the user number attached to the file name. If either Romeo or Juliet asks for a listing of the files on the disc, with the DIR command, they will get a display of only the files that they (or someone else) had created while they were logged-on as user number 1, in Romeo's case, or user number 2 in Juliet's.

Protecting files
- user numbers

Even though there may be other files on the disc, the files will not be listed and they will not be allowed access to them (unless they log-on again with the appropriate user number).

Try this:

1 Key-in: **USER 1 {RETURN}**. Notice the new system prompt.

2 Key-in: **DIR {RETURN}**. You probably got the message **No File** for your pains, yet you know there are lots of files on the disc.

The files on your disc have all been created under user number 0 (zero) so they are not available to anyone logged-on under a different user number, unless you take some other action. Program files created under User Number 0 can be made available to other users by turning the files into System Files. (See the previous section.)

3 Now key-in: **USER 0 {RETURN}** to set things back to normal.

Setting passwords

If you want to restrict access to certain discs or files, you can set up password access - not only to prevent access, but to control the operations that can be performed when access is given. There are three modes of protection: Read, Write and Delete.

The first thing you need to do when setting up a password is to switch on the password protection for the drive.

Note

When you are setting up, or using, passwords they appear on the screen so you need to be sure nobody else can read the screen while you are working with them.

1   Start by putting your working copy of the CP/M disc in drive A:. Then key-in:
  SET A: [PROTECT=ON, PASSWORD=[PASSWORD]] and tap {RETURN}. (This command merely switches the password protection on. You use a password for this to prevent other users turning the protection off. When you use this command, don't forget the password!)

Setting passwords

You now have three 'modes' of protection which you specify as follows. To guard against:

- Reading, copying, changing, deleting or renaming = READ

- Changing, deleting or renaming = WRITE

- Deleting = DELETE

If you copy a password protected file to a different disc using the same name, the same password and protection mode will be maintained. If you give the copy a new password, by adding ';' and the new password after the new filename, the protection will be set to READ.

3 To set the password for, say, PIP.COM, key-in:
SET PIP.COM [PASSWORD=[PASSWORD], PROTECT= [MODE]] and {RETURN}.

Note

Groups of files can be copied only if they share the same password and if you set the Default Password to this password first by keying-in: **SET [DEFAULT = [PASSWORD]]**.

We had better switch the password off again, so:

1 Key-in: **SET A: [PROTECT=OFF]** and tap {RETURN}. The computer will ask you for a password before it will set the protection off, so key-in your password and tap {RETURN}.

Using SET on drives and discs

You can use the SET program to specify attributes for discs and disc drives as well as the file settings we have seen so far.

Setting the attributes of a disc drive

If you want to stop other people writng to your discs – to protect your precious data – you can make one (or all) of your drives 'Read Only' devices. For example:

1   Key-in: **SET A: [RO]{RETURN}**.

Now, if you or anyone else tries to write to that drive CP/M will not let you – even if you change disc. If you want to test this out:

2   Key-in: **REN PROFILE.BAK=PROFILE.SUB{RETURN}**.

You will see CP/M try to carry out the command, but then it will stop and display the message, '**ERROR: Drive read only**'. So you can see for yourself that drive A: is now a Read Only drive, but beware! As soon as you reboot the system, drive A: will go back to its default setting of RW. So we may as well set it back before we carry on.

3   Key-in: **SET A: [RW]{RETURN}**.

Using SET on drives and discs

One way of keeping track of your files is to put different types of files on different data discs. For example, you could have one disc for general correspondence, one for quotations, one for invoices and one for begging letters to the bank. You can then label the discs appropriately. You can take this principle a bit further if you name the disc itself. In other words, you can have a paper label stuck to the casing of the disc and you can have a magnetic label stored on the medium inside the casing. Here's how to create a magnetic label. (Sorry, but you'll have to research the use of paper labels for yourself!)

Let us assume that we are labelling a disc which holds letters to the bank.

1 Take your CP/M start-up disc out of drive A: and replace it with a data disc. Key-in:
   SET [NAME=FORGIVE.ME]{RETURN}.

The rules for naming discs are the same as those for naming files – i.e. the first part, the Name, must be no more than 8 characters in length. If you use a Type extension, it must be preceded by a dot (fullstop) and it must contain no more than three characters.

The SET command confirms the label you have put on this disc and it tells you the settings for various other features.

Using SET on drives and discs

Note

You can get CP/M to date and time-stamp alterations to this disc, but for this to work properly you will have to set the time and date each time you start-up CP/M.

If you have a 9000 series machine and you want to check the magnetic label of a disc, it makes things a lot easier if you put a copy of SHOW.COM onto your M: drive. If you have an 8000 series machine you will already have a copy of SHOW.COM on the memory drive.

1 Put your CP/M start-up disc in drive A: and key-in:
PIP M:=A:SHOW.COM[V] and **{RETURN}**. Then, when you get the **A>** prompt again, put your data disc back into drive A: ready for the next command.

Notes

a. If you have a 9000 series machine, this PIP command may be one you would like to add to the PROFILE.SUB file, if someone hasn't already done so! That way you will always have a copy of SHOW.COM to hand.

b. The '[V]' at the end of the command line ensures that PIP verifies that the file has been copied correctly.

Using SET on drives and discs

Now, no matter what machine you have we should be ready to check the label of our disc in drive A:.

1 Key-in: **SHOW [LABEL]{RETURN}** and watch the screen.

SHOW duly provides you with the label name for the disc as well as the summary of other settings you saw just now. But what happens if the disc in the drive does not have a label?

1 Put your CP/M start-up disc in drive A: and tap the **COPY** key (or PASTE or ALT-W) to recall the last command you keyed-in and then tap **{RETURN}**.

SHOW responds with an error message, telling you, '**No directory label exists on drive A:**'.

I think you'll agree that labelling your discs magnetically offers you another way of keeping track of your work files. It is pretty easy to do and yet it can save you a lot of time when you are searching for a particular file.

Chapter 3
Managing Discs

Checklist - looking after discs

I make no apology for repeating this checklist here.

- Make a back-up of a Program Disc as soon as you get it. If you have not made copies of the PCW's master discs, do so now! (See the section on 'Copying Discs'.)

- Work with your back-up discs not your master discs

- You should back-up discs at the end of each working session

- Back-up each file as soon as you finish working with it

- Always store master discs and back-ups in separate boxes. and preferably in separate rooms. Always store discs in a dust proof container of some kind and at room temperatures

- Never touch the magnetic surfaces of the disc

- Never switch the computer on or off with a disc in a drive

- Try to keep data files separate from program files

- Unless you need to save information on your program disc, it is a good idea to write protect it before you start work. Push the 'write protect tab' (in the top left hand corner of the disc) down towards the letter A or B

- Make sure that you establish a routine procedure for identifying discs (and what's on them) - i.e. devise an index of some kind.

Resetting (rebooting) the PCW

1 Start by getting your working copy of the disc labelled 'CP/M Plus' and put it in drive A:.

2 With your left hand, hold down **SHIFT** and **EXTRA** then with your right hand, tap the key labelled **EXIT**. You will see the PCW go through its CP/M start up sequence.

Holding down **SHIFT** + **EXTRA**, then tapping the **EXIT** key is the procedure you use to 'Reset', or 'Reboot' your computer.

3 The Reset procedure overrides anything the computer is doing at the time, but be careful with it, because resetting the PCW involves flushing out the memory and the memory drive (drive M:). So if you had been working on something in drive M: and you had not saved it on disc, you would lose it forever. Also, with certain software packages, you might scramble the data files if you do not close down properly before resetting!

Note

As you know, if you reset with the CP/M Plus disc in the drive, you will get access to the CP/M Plus Operating System. But if you reset with the LocoScript disc in the drive, then you will start-up LocoScript. You can set up 'autoboot discs' like this for other programs, as we shall see later.

Creating a (data) disc

It is a good idea to keep programs and data on separate discs; if nothing else, you will be able to get more data on a disc if it is dedicated to one job!

Before you can use a new disc to hold data files (or program files for that matter) you will have to go through a procedure to prepare the disc for its job. When you get a brand new disc it is simply a frail sheet of plastic material which has a thin magnetic coating. Before you can use the disc to store information of any kind, you will have to 'mark out' a pattern of tracks on the surface. These tracks hold the magnetic 'pigeon-holes' for the data and they have to be laid out accurately in a very precise format. That is why the preparation procedure is known as 'FORMATTING' the disc.

FORMATTING is very easy to do - dangerously easy!

Have your CP/M start-up disc to hand as well as your brand new disc.

1   Start by getting your working copy of the disc labelled 'CP/M Plus' and put it in drive A:.

2   With your left hand, hold down the keys labelled **SHIFT** and **EXTRA**, then with your right hand, tap the key labelled **EXIT** to reset your PCW.

We want to FORMAT a disc and to do that you need to use a program called DISCKIT.COM which is on your CP/M start-up disc (which should still be in drive A:).

Creating a (data) disc

3   Key-in: **DISCKIT {RETURN}**.

The PCW responds by running the DISCKIT program. You'll see a message on screen telling you how many disc drives DISCKIT has found and asking you to remove the disc(s) and then press a key.

4   Remove the disc(s) and then tap the **SPACEBAR**.

DISCKIT displays a 'menu' which offers you four options. Reading from the top, they are: COPY (tap the key labelled f6/f5), FORMAT (tap f4/f3), VERIFY (tap f2/f1), or tap the EXIT key to leave DISCKIT.

5   We want to FORMAT a disc, so tap the **f4/f3** key.

Single drive machine:
You will be asked to provide the disc which is to be formatted.

Twin drive 8000 series machine:
The second drive on the **PCW8000** series machines is different from the A: drive – it has a different capacity and a different format, so DISCKIT needs to know which format you want it to create. So, you will also be asked to tell DISCKIT which drive will hold the disc to be formatted. **Format the disc in drive A:**

If you have a **PCW9512** with two floppy disc drives, I recommend that you get into the habit of putting the disc in drive B: - with side 1 uppermost - and then nominating that drive.

Creating a (data) disc

6   When you are ready, put your new disc in the appropriate drive and tap-in the appropriate drive name, if asked. Then tap the letter **Y** to start the formatting process (or tap any other key if you decide not to go ahead).

You will see disckit keep a count as it lays down the tracks (the numbering on computers starts from 0) on the surface of the disc.

When DISCKIT has finished, the disc will be formatted and it will be ready to hold data, or programs.

Close down DISCKIT, by removing the disc from the drive and tapping **ANY KEY** on the main part of the keyboard. Then tap the **EXIT** key.

You now have an empty but useable disc which you can use for any purpose you like, so let us look at some refinements you can implement if you decide to use it to hold programs.

Booting automatically into a program

One additional refinement to the process of creating working discs is to make the new disc automatically boot into a program when you start up, or when you reset/reboot the system). To do this you have to put a copy of the CP/M operating system file, SUBMIT.COM and an amended version of the file PROFILE.SUB on your new disc as follows. This procedure assumes that your CP/M disc has PROFILE.SUB on it (see Chapter 1).

Notes

a. If you want to be able to boot your PCW with your new disc it must have on it a copy of the CP/M system. We saw earlier that this is held in a file called J14CPM3.EMS. You have a copy of this file on your copy CP/M disc, so we must copy it over from your CP/M disc and put it on your new disc. Similarly we must copy PROFILE.SUB and SUBMIT.COM from the CP/M disc onto your new disc.

b. Remember that CP/M looks for a file called PROFILE.SUB when it starts up. It does not know, or care, what is in the file. It will simply implement any commands it finds. So we can quite happily put a file called PROFILE.SUB on our new disc and we can put any commands we like into that file.

Booting automatically into a program

Notes

c. We have to remember that the files on our new disc will be copies of the originals on our copy CP/M disc, which we write protected earlier on. So, we will not be able to edit any of the files unless we make it a Read Write file. We may as well set all the files to be Read Write.

1 Start by getting your working copy of the disc labelled 'CP/M Plus' and put it in drive A:.

2 Key-in **SET *.*[RW]{RETURN}**.

3 Just in case, we shall reset the PCW before we go any further: **SHIFT+EXTRA**, and with your right hand, tap the key labelled **EXIT**.

Now, for this example we need to clear some space in the memory drive. So:

4 Key-in: **ERA M:*.COM{RETURN}** and the letter **Y**.

It will look as though nothing has happened, but try keying-in DIR M:{RETURN} if you would like to check things out.

Booting automatically into a program

5   At the **A>** prompt, key-in: **PIP {RETURN}** and, when PIP displays its usual helpful asterisk prompt, key-in: **M:=J14CPM3.EMS{RETURN}**.

6   Now key-in:. **M:=SUBMIT.COM{RETURN}**. Finally key-in: **M:=PROFILE.SUB{RETURN}**.

Note

At this stage of the procedure you have in memory the programs you need to create a disc which will boot the system. But we want to go one step further and get it to start-up a program automatically. So we are still short of two things: Firstly, the program we want to start-up, and secondly, the start-up command itself.

Just for the purposes of this exercise we will use RPED as the program we want to boot into. Now RPED is a program written in the language BASIC so, in order to run the program, we will need a copy of the BASIC language as well as the necessary RPED files on our automatic start-up disc. So,

7   With PIP still running, key-in: **M:=BASIC.*{RETURN}** and then **M:=RPED.*{RETURN}**.

Leave PIP running!

Booting automatically into a program

8 Take your CP/M disc from drive A: and replace it with your new disc. Then key-in: **A:=M:*.*{RETURN}** to transfer copies of all the files from the memory drive to your new (empty) disc. Then tap **{RETURN}** once more to close down PIP.

You should have the **A>** prompt on screen and you are now ready to alter PROFILE.SUB to work with your new program. Isn't it fortunate we copied RPED onto our new disc!

Booting automatically into a program - editing PROFILE.SUB

1   Key-in **RPED {RETURN}**. (If you don't know what RPED is, see Chapter 1.)

2   At the RPED menu screen, tap **f1**. With your new disc in the drive, key-in **PROFILE.SUB {RETURN}**. The destination file is the same as the source file in this case, so tap **{RETURN}**

What you will see on screen are the instructions that CP/M follows when you start up, or boot up, your system. It includes copying certain files to memory, drive M: and directions on the sequence in which instructions are to be carried out. What we must do now is to get rid of the commands we don't want, and then you need to add the start up instruction for RPED. Here we shall delete all the lines.

3   Tap the **CUT** key once to delete the line the cursor is on, then repeat the CUT process for all the other lines in the file.

You can see from this action that there was actually no need to copy PROFILE.SUB across from the CP/M disc (you could have simply created a new one here). But I thought it better to show you this procedure in case you want to create boot discs which do implement essentially the same start-up routine.

Booting automatically into a program- editing PROFILE.SUB

Note

Remember, when you are working with RPED, the DELete, ALT+Delete and CUT keys can be used to remove text. To insert text, you move the cursor to the line where you want the text to appear, hold down ALT and tap the DOWN ARROW key if you need to insert a line and key-in the text. Use the arrow keys to move to the next line if need be. The {RETURN} key simply moves the cursor to the start of the next line.

4 Now key-in: **BASIC RPED** and tap **{RETURN}** (the RPED start-up command). This completes the changes we need to make, so tap the **EXIT** key to return to the Menu Screen and **EXIT** again to go back to the system prompt.

5 With your new working disc still in drive A:, hold down **SHIFT** and **EXTRA** and tap **EXIT** and the system should load up RPED automatically. If it doesn't, use RPED to check and amend the PROFILE.SUB file, then try again.

6 When the automatic boot disc works properly, tap **EXIT** to leave RPED. Now that you have seen the principle and assuming you don't want this disc to always start-up with RPED, I would advise you to clear PROFILE.SUB from the disc now. Key-in: **ERA PROFILE.SUB{RETURN}**.

Finding out what is on a disc

When you start up the PCW under LocoScript, the screen displays a complete list of the files on your disc - separated into groups. If you change the disc in the drive and then tap the f7/f8 key, that display will change to tell you which files and groups are on the new disc. So when you are word processing it is very easy, but perhaps a bit cumbersome to find what you are looking for.

But what happens when you decide to use the PCW for something other than word processing and you want to keep your filing system up to date? Or if you have simply lost track of a file you need? Is there a quicker way to get a listing of the files on a disc? Well, yes there is. Let's assume that your machine is already switched on.

1   Start by getting your working copy of the CP/M Plus disc and put it in the A: drive.

2   With your left hand, hold own the keys labelled **SHIFT** and **EXTRA**. Then with your right hand, tap the key labelled **EXIT**.

3   We want to get a list or 'directory' of the files on the CP/M disc, so key-in: **DIR** and tap **{RETURN}**. You will see a list of the file names appear on screen.

You have seen all this before, but we haven't yet analysed the directory display to see what it tells you.

Finding out what is on a disc

Note that you are given a directory of the disc in drive A: (you can tell that because each line of filenames is preceded by 'A:'). There are three things to notice here:

- When you start up under CP/M, the computer assumes (in default of any contrary instruction from you) that any command you key-in applies to the disc in drive A: (in other words, drive A: is its 'default drive') and that's why you got a **DIR**ectory of the disc in drive A:

- You can elect to work on another drive, by simply keying-in the identifying letter (followed by a colon) of the drive you want and then tapping {RETURN}, e.g. **M: {RETURN}** or **m: {RETURN}**. This process is known as 'logging-on' to a drive.

- You can get a directory for another disc drive without having to log-on to that drive. For example, if you now want to find out which files are in the memory drive (drive M:), but you don't want to log to that drive, key-in: **DIR M:{RETURN}**.

4 (!! If you have a twin drive machine, put a disc in the second drive now!!) Try keying-in: **DIR B:** and now tap **{RETURN}**. If you have a twin drive machine you will get a list of the files on the disc in drive B:. If you have the single drive machine, see the next page.

DIR variants (options)

5 On a single drive machine, when you ask for a directory of drive B: you hit a slight logical problem, you have only one drive - and that's called drive A:! But the PCW can cope. The screen prompts you to provide a disc for B:.

What it means is: 'For the time being, let's pretend that your drive A: is called drive B:, so put another disc in the drive then tap the SPACEBAR to let me know when you've done it.' (Clever isn't it!?)

6 Now, normally, you would do as you are told. But let us cheat a bit, don't change the disc. Just tap the **SPACEBAR**. And away goes the PCW, giving you a directory of what it thinks is drive B:. Again, you can tell because each row of filenames is now preceded by 'B:'. (So it's really quite dumb!)

The DIR command has other variants or enhancements which you might find useful, so it is worth looking at them now. The first thing to realise is that you'll need a copy of the program DIR.COM to use the enhancements to the built-in DIR command. If you have a copy of our PROFILE.SUB file on the CP/M boot disc you will have a copy of DIR.COM on your memory drive. So, let's try some commands.

1 Key-in: **DIR M:{RETURN}** and then try keying-in: **DIR [SIZE] M:{RETURN}**.

Compare the displays and you will see they are different.

DIR variants (options)

The response to the first command is a simple list of files. The second is more comprehensive. You can see that the DIR command program scans the directory, then it sorts the files and only then does it list the files. Notice they are in alphabetical order and each file name now has a number after it. For example, 'PIP.COM 9k'.

Note

That number tells you the size of the file in question – in this example 9 kilobytes (or, roughly 9 thousand characters of information. In fact a kilobyte is 1024 bytes, and you can think of a byte as representing a single character. So the program PIP.COM takes up 9,216 bytes of space on the disc (assuming it is exactly 9k in size).

You also get a lot more information about the disc after the list of files. Now let us try another variant of this command.

2   Key-in: **DIR [EXCLUDE] *.COM{RETURN}**.

This time you get another list of files, in alphabetical order and with the size of the file appended. But, as you can see, the list is a lot shorter because you have asked CP/M to exclude or omit all the .COM files from the listing.

If you have a twin drive machine make sure you have a disc in both the disc drives.

DIR variants (options)

3   Key-in: **DIR [DRIVE=ALL]{RETURN}**, to get a sorted list for all your drives. You may have to tap {RETURN} to see it all.

You can even combine the DIR options, like this:

4   Key-in: **DIR ????.COM [EXCLUDE,DRIVE=ALL]{RETURN}**.

What we have asked for here is a sorted directory of all the drives, but excluding .COM files whose names have four or less characters.

Working with system files. For the next couple of commands I want to look at, we shall have to get some more files onto the memory drive and play around with the ones already there, so:

1   Key-in: **PIP M:=PROFILE.*{RETURN}**.

2   Then key-in: **SET M:*.COM [SYS]{RETURN}**.

3   Lastly, key-in: **SET M:*.COM [RO]{RETURN}**.

The first command puts a couple of files on M: which are not .COM files (i.e. PROFILE.SUB and PROFILE.ENG), the second sets all the .COM files on M: to be system files and the third makes those system files Read Only files. (N.B. You could have combined the last two commands by keying-in: SET M:*.COM[SYS,RO].)

DIR variants (options)

Now we are ready to carry on looking at the DIR options I mentioned just now.

1 Start by keying in **DIR M:{RETURN}** and note the display you get now.

You should have a very short list of files, but notice also that below the list it tells you that 'SYSTEM FILE(S) EXIST' on the disc in question. How do you get to see what they are?

2 Key-in: **DIR M: [SYS]{RETURN}**. Notice, you get a list of the system files on drive M: and that list is sorted into alphabetical order and it shows the sizes of the files. You can shorten this command, but you get a slightly different result. Key-in: **DIRS M:{RETURN}**. This time you get a normal type of listing, of just the system files, but you also get a message telling you that 'NON-SYSTEM FILE(S) EXIST'.

You may want to find out which of the files on a disc are Read Only and which are Read Write. Here's how.

3 Key-in **DIR M: [RO]{RETURN}**.

Not surprisingly you get the same listing you had just now when you asked for a list of SYS files – they happen to be the same files in this case. So let us try something else.

93

DIR variants (options)

4 Key-in: **DIR M: [RW]{RETURN}**.

This display is of the same type as you had just now, but the contents of the list are different.

Note

In particular, compare the two lots of information which appear below the files lists. You will see that the 'Used/Max Dir Entries For Drive M:' are the same, but all the other details are different. These last items in the blocks of information tell you how many of the discs 64 slots for file names you have used up, the other items tell you how much space is taken up by the types of file in question.

Now for a single command which will get you all the information you need about the files on a disc.

1 Key-in: **DIR M: [FULL]{RETURN}**.

This command causes the PCW to tell you the names of the files, the sizes and the attributes (whether a file is Sys or Dir and whether it is RO or RW). It also gives you a breakdown of how the disc space is used. Notice that the files are listed in alphabetical order.

DIR variants (options)

If several people use your PCW under different user numbers, there is one more DIR command which might be useful to you. But before I can show it to you we shall have to create a file under a different user number. See the section in Chapter 2 headed 'Sending information from the keyboard and creating a new file on disc'

1   Key-in **M:{RETURN}** to log to the memory drive. Now key-in: **USER 7{RETURN}** to log-on as user number 7. (I'm asuming that you do not already have a user who logs on as number 7! - Not that it actually matters here.) Notice the amended system prompt.

2   Key-in: **PIP MYFILE.TXT=CON:{RETURN}**. Next, key-in: **This is a PIP file.** followed by **ALT-J** and **ALT-Z**.

3   Next, get a directory of the disc, key-in: **DIR{RETURN}**. You will see that only one file is listed – the one in 'user area' 7.

How do you find out which are files in other user areas?

1   Key-in: **DIR [USER=ALL]{RETURN}** and watch the screen.

I think you'll agree, the DIR variants we have examined in this section of the book should equip you to track down a file, no matter how elusive it may be. Happy hunting!

Log back to user number 0 (zero) by keying-in: **USER 0{RETURN}**.

Checking the space on a disc

You can get a lot of information on a disc, but there is a limit. Before you start what looks like being a lengthy job which will generate a lot of information, it is a good idea to check that there will be enough room on the disc.

The precise amount you need will vary with the job you are doing, but for word processing, if you work on a maximum of 65 characters per line, with 55 lines per page (for 11 inch continuous paper) you can see that you will have to allow for roughly 65 times 55, or 3575 characters for each page. (In fact, an average of 2.5 to 3 thousand characters per page is usually close enough). So now you know how much space you need, how do you find out how much you've got?

Well you need the CP/M program called SHOW.COM which is on your CP/M disc and, if your boot disc has PROFILE.SUB on it, it will be put on the M: drive when you start-up the system.

1   Put your working copy of the CP/M disc in drive A:. If you have two drive slots also put any other disc in the right hand drive.

2   If you have RESET your system since working through the previous section you will need to repeat the procedures in the last three and a bit pages – from the sub-heading **'Working with system files'**, before you work through this section.

Checking the space on a disc

3   At the system prompt, key-in: **SHOW B: {RETURN}**.

With a twin drive system, the PCW goes ahead, but with the single drive system you'll be prompted to provide a disc for B: first. For now, just tap the **SPACEBAR** as if you had swapped discs.

The SHOW command tells the PCW to look at the disc in the drive you have specified (B: in this case) and report on how much free space remains. You should see a display which says something like: **B: RW, Space 100k** (though if you have a PCW8256 the number will be a lot smaller).

The 'RW' signifies that you can 'read' from this disc and 'write' to it - i.e. use it normally.

'Space 100k' tells you that you have enough room to fit another 100 thousand ('100k') 'bytes' on the disc in drive B: (or, with a single drive machine, what the PCW thinks is drive B:). What about the others?

1   Key-in the command word **SHOW** on its own and tap **{RETURN}**.

If you have a single drive machine, the computer will beep and ask you to put the disc for A: into the drive and then tap any key. Just tap the **SPACEBAR** again.

SHOW - variants (options)

This time the PCW tells you how much space is left on each of the discs on your system. If you have a single drive machine, notice that the PCW includes an amount for the nonexistent drive B:.

The SHOW command is designed to give you information about your discs and your drives. For example, if you want to find out how many of your 64 directory entries you have left on the disc:

1   Key-in **SHOW [DIR]{RETURN}** and SHOW will tell you.

If you want to know the characteristics of your drives:

1   Key-in: **SHOW [DRIVE]{RETURN}**, for the A: drive and key-in: **SHOW M:[DRIVE]{RETURN}**, for the M: drive.

Compare the characteristics of the two drives (and, incidentally any other on your machine).

If you want to find out which user numbers exist on a disc (in our case only on M:), then:

1   Key-in: **SHOW M:[USERS]{RETURN}**.

SHOW will display firstly your current user number, zero, then the active (user) files, zero and seven, and then the number of files in each user area, probably ten and one.

Making a duplicate copy of a disc

We have already seen that you should make a back-up of any disc that you are using and that, at least with program discs, you should use that back-up disc to work from.

Note for PCW9512 users

If you are using a PCW9512 and the disc you are using was created for the PCW9512, you can follow the procedure described in this section. If you are wanting to use a program written for the PCW8256 or PCW8512 then you will need the special facility '8000COPY' which is described in the next section.

You will need a new or blank disc for this procedure.

1 Reset your machine with **SHIFT+EXTRA** and **EXIT**.

When you get the **A>** prompt on screen, CP/M is ready to accept your commands. We want to copy a disc and to do that you need to use a program called DISCKIT which is on your CP/M Plus disc (which should still be in drive A:).

2 Key-in: **DISCKIT {RETURN}**.

The PCW responds by running the DISCKIT program. You'll see a message on screen telling you how many disc drives DISCKIT has found and asking you to remove the disc(s) and then press a key.

Making a duplicate copy of a disc

3 Push the button on the front of the disc drive to release the disc and then tap the **SPACEBAR**.

DISCKIT displays a 'menu' which offers you four options. Reading from the top: COPY (tap the key labelled 'f6/f5' , FORMAT (tap f4/f3), VERIFY (f2/f1), or tap the EXIT key to leave DISCKIT.

4 We want to copy a disc, so tap the **f6/f5** key.

Single Drive Machine: DISCKIT asks you to put the disc you want to read - copy **from** - in the drive and then tap the letter **Y**.

Double Drive: DISCKIT asks you which drive you want to read - copy **from** - (tap f4/f3 for drive A: or f2/f1 for drive B:). Next you will be asked to specify which drive you want to 'write' to - copy **to** (tap f4/f3 for drive A: - f2/f1 for drive B:).

5 **Single Drive:** Put the disc you want to copy **from** into the drive, then tap the letter **Y**. Have your new or blank disc ready.

Double Drive: (Recommended procedure) Put the disc you want to copy **from** in drive A: and then tap **f4/f3**. Put the disc you want to copy **to** in drive B: and tap **f2/f1**, then tap the letter **Y**.

Making a duplicate copy of a disc

DISCKIT will now copy your disc for you. If you have a single drive machine (or if you had elected to read from one drive and write to the same one) DISCKIT will prompt you to swap discs at the appropriate times.

Notes

a. If the disc you are writing to is brand new you will see a message telling you that DISCKIT will 'format' while it is copying (see the section headed, 'Creating a (data) disc').

b. If you are working with a single disc drive DISCKIT will format and copy a disc in three parts, each part copies a block of tracks. In the top left hand corner of the screen DISCKIT keeps a count of where it has got to during the copy process. You will see it read from and write to 'tracks'. When it has finished, the screen will ask you to remove the disc(s) and tap a key.

c. If, during the copy process, you are asked to swap discs and you put the wrong disc in the drive, or put the right disc in upside down, DISCKIT will spot your mistake and ask you to rectify it.

d. If, during the copy process, you do not push the disc home securely in the drive, DISCKIT will think that the disc is missing altogether and it will prompt you to provide the right disc and then tap R to retry the activity (or tap C to cancel).

101

Making a duplicate copy of a disc

6 When prompted by DISCKIT, remove the disc(s) and tap the **SPACEBAR**.

DISCKIT asks if you want to make another copy.

7 If yes, tap the Y key and repeat the process. If no, tap the **SPACEBAR**.

DISCKIT displays its main menu again (the one with 4 options).

8 Tap **EXIT** to leave DISCKIT. Don't forget to label your new disc.

PCW9512: copying a disc from 8000 format

PCW 9000 series users

The floppy discs that you use with your PCW9512 look the same as those used with the PCW8256 and PCW8512. They are, however, formatted differently, i.e. the number of tracks laid down on the surface of the disc electronically is greater and so is the capacity of the disc, c720k as opposed to c180k for the A: drive on an 8000 series machine.

This means that you can store a great deal more information on the disc and therefore work more efficiently. But it also means that if you want to use a program which has been created in the 8000 format or if you want to use work that you originally set up on an 8000 series machine you need to copy this to a disc which you can use on your PCW9512.

On your CP/M disc you will find a file called '8000COPY' which is the one you use instead of DISCKIT to copy a disc.

Before you can start the copy procedure you will need a disc which is formatted for the PCW9512, ready to receive the information you are going to copy. If your disc is not already formatted for the 9512, follow the steps described in the section titled, 'Formatting a new disc'.

1 Start by getting your working copy of the disc labelled 'CP/M Plus' and put it in the disc drive (the left hand one if you have two disc drive slots).

PCW9512: copying a disc from 8000 format

2   With your CP/M Plus disc in the floppy drive, at the 'A' prompt, key-in: **8000COPY {RETURN}**.

You will see some text appear on screen, explaining the 8000COPY procedure. You have the option to create a disc which will start CP/M Plus automatically when you switch your machine on and insert the new copy disc. Since this is the most straightforward option, we shall follow it through here. The text then reminds you that you must have a formatted disc ready to copy to, and it displays the warning, for single disc drive machines 'This will erase all files on drive M:'.

Note

If you do have a single drive machine and if you have any information on drive M: which you have not yet saved to disc, copy that information to disc now **before** you start the 8000COPY procedure! I.e. tap **N** in response to 'Do you want to continue' and this will take you back to the A> prompt.

3   To proceed with 8000COPY, tap **Y** in response to 'Do you want to continue (Y/N)?'.

4   You are then asked if you want to make the destination disc – the disc you are copying to – 'bootable', so it will start up CP/M automatically. Tap **Y**.

PCW9512: copying a disc from 8000 format

5   Make sure your CP/M disc is still in drive A: and tap the **SPACEBAR**. If you have a **single drive machine**, the system reads the CP/M system file and erases all files from drive M:. If you have a **twin drive machine** you should insert your destination disc in drive B:, the right hand drive slot, and the copy procedure will proceed without using Drive M:.

6   If you have a **single drive machine**, remove the CP/M Plus disc and insert the disc you are copying from, the one which is in normal, i.e. 180K or 8000 format, into Drive A:.

7   If the disc contains LocoScript files, tap **Y**, if not, tap **N** and the copying will begin. You can follow the progress on screen.

8   When prompted, remove the source disc and insert your destination disc and tap the **SPACEBAR**.

When copying is complete, you will be asked 'Do you have another normal capacity disc to copy?'. If the answer is Yes, tap **Y** and continue until all copying is complete, then tap **N**. All files on drive M: are erased and you return to the A> prompt.

You should be able to copy the contents of four normal capacity discs to the higher capacity discs. In each case you will be asked if the disc contains LocoScript files. Tap **Y** or **N** as appropriate.

PCW9512: copying a disc from 8000 format

If you attempt to copy a file which already exists on the destination disc, a warning message appears on screen and you have the option to overwrite the original version or not as you wish.

To use your new disc:

1 Reboot the system by holding down **SHIFT+EXTRA** and tapping **EXIT**. To start the program you want, key-in the appropriate instruction as shown in your program documentation.

Chapter 4
Managing Hardware

Setting the PCW's clock

1   If you have an **8000 series machine,** put a copy of your **Disc 3 'Programming Utilities'** disc in drive A:
If you have a **9512**, put a copy of your **CP/M Plus** disc in drive A:.

2   Key-in: **DATE{RETURN}**.

On my systems (8000 and 9000 series), the PCWs respond by displaying: '**Wed 12/15/82 01:59:58**'. The first part of the display gives the date the CP/M operating system was created (even though one is version 1.4 and the other is version 2.1, they both have the same date) – Wednesday the 15th of December 1982, in English – The second half of the display is the length of time the machines have been switched on since I started work today – just two seconds short of two hours. (It's about time I had a rest!) But, before I slope off, let's update the computer and tell it today's date (in American format) and the exact time. The actual time and date don't matter for this exercise, so we'll lie to it; we'll say it is 11.00 o'clock in the morning on the Ides Of March 1999.

1   Tap the **COPY** key to repeat the last command you keyed-in (**DATE**), add a **SPACE**, then **03/15/99 11:00:00{RETURN}**.

2   The PCW will prompt you to '**Strike** (a) **key to set time**'. Keep an ear on Big Ben, or the church clock, or your chiming pocket watch and on the first stroke of eleven o'clock, tap **{RETURN}**.

109

Checking the PCW's clock

Now you have set the PCW's clock it will keep track of the time and date until you switch it off again. You will have to reset the clock each time you start-up the system.

Let's see how accurate it is.

1 Tap the **COPY** key to recall the last command you keyed in and use the **←DEL** key to erase the time and the date, leaving just the word '**DATE**' on the command line. Then tap **{RETURN}**.

You should discover that the 1999 Ides Of March fall (or fell, if this book is still around in late 1999) on a Monday.

Note

Just for a bit of fun, if you want to find out what day your birthday falls on next year (or later this year) all you have to do is key-in 'DATE' followed by your birth date (in American format 'month/day/year' – using two digits for each) followed by a time, say 1 o'clock in the morning, then tap {RETURN} twice to set the clock. Then you simply give the DATE command again and the PCW will tell you the relevant day of the week. I've just found out that my birthday falls on a Thursday next year. That's interesting isn't it!?

Oh! It's not! Oh well ....

Putting screen and printer outputs into disc files

In Chapter 2 we saw that you can redirect the normal outputs from a disc file and from the screen to create new disc files and to get printouts. There, we examined how you achieve these ends with PIP – CP/M's 'Peripheral Interchange Programme'. You have another command at your disposal which enables you to do very similar things. That command is 'PUT'.

If you have one of the original 8000 series machines, the command program PUT.COM is on your disc 3, but with other PCWs it is on the CP/M disc. You may never want to use PUT, but it is worth having a look at it just in case you can think of some applications which suit your way of working.

1   Place the appropriate disc in drive A: and key-in: **PUT{RETURN}**.

PUT confirms that it will direct the output from the console (the screen) to a file on disc and it asks you to key-in the name of the file you want it to create. We shall get a directory of the disc in drive A: and we'll save that output in a file on M: called MYDIR.

2   Key-in: **M:MYDIR{RETURN}** to create the empty file on drive M: ready to receive the screen output.

Again, PUT tells you what it will do.

Putting screen and printer outputs into disc files

3   Key-in: **DIR [SIZE]{RETURN}**. (If there is more than one screen 'page' of file names, you may have to tap the {RETURN} key.)

The PCW scans the directory and produces a display of all the files on the disc in drive A:. They are listed in alphabetical order and the size of each appears next to its name. Now let's see if the PUT command worked.

4   Key-in: **TYPE M:MYDIR [NO PAGE]{RETURN}**.

And you should get an action replay of the results you got on screen a few moments ago. Now try this:

5   Tap the **COPY** key to recall the last command you keyed-in (TYPE M:MYDIR [NO PAGE]). Check that the printer has some paper in it and is ready to go and tap **ALT-P** and then **{RETURN}** to get a hard-copy (printout) of the contents of the file M:MYDIR.

You have ended up with a disc file and a printout of the directory of the disc in drive A:. You can get very similar end results by using PUT in a slightly different way.

Putting screen and printer outputs into disc files

1 Key-in: **PUT PRINTER OUTPUT TO FILE M:DIRFILE** and then tap the **{RETURN}** key.

This creates the empty file on drive M: ready for the printer output

2 Next key-in **DIR M: [SIZE]{RETURN}** and tap **ALT-P**. Then tap **{RETURN}** and, when you get the **A>** prompt back, tap **ALT-P** again.

If you look at the printout or the screen display of the directory for drive M:, you will see there is a file called DIRFILE on the drive, but you'll notice that it has zero size.

3 Tap the **COPY** key to recall the last command you keyed-in (**DIR M: [SIZE]**) and then tap **{RETURN}**.

Here you will see that DIRFILE now has a size. The original display and the printout were generated before the PUT command had directed the printer output into the file; that's why the file had zero size.

So you have seen how to use PUT, as it were, to do one task at a time – i.e. to get one batch of screen or printer output into a file. But how do you get a sequence of outputs into a single file? For example, let's say you had written the RPED editing program and you wanted to generate printed versions of its various screen displays so you can include them in the users handbook. How would you do it?

Putting screen and printer outputs into disc files

1   Start by keying-in: **PUT CONSOLE OUTPUT TO FILE M:RPEDOPS [SYSTEM]{RETURN}**.

The [SYSTEM] option in the command is the one which leaves PUT switched on all the time. So when we finish this job we shall have to remember to switch it off again.

Note

The RPED program contains lots of control codes to highlight bits of the text, position other bits of text in precise locations on screen, etc. The file we generate will contain these control codes, not the end result of the codes! But the fact that we get anything at all in our file will illustrate the point I am trying to make here.

2   **If you have one of the original 8000 series machines**, take your disc 3 from the drive and replace it with the working copy of your CP/M start-up disc.

3   Key-in: **RPED{RETURN}** and watch the screen. When you get the RPED opening screen, take your CP/M disc from drive A: and replace it with a data disc.

4   Tap the **f3/f4** key, then key-in: **ANYNAME{RETURN}** to get to the editing screen. Then key-in: **NOW IS THE TIME**.

Putting screen and printer outputs into disc files

5 Then simply tap the **EXIT** key **twice** to leave RPED.

6 Remove the data disc from drive A: and replace it with the disc which holds the PUT command program (disc 3 on the original 8000 series PCWs). Then key-in **PUT CONSOLE OUTPUT TO CONSOLE{RETURN}** to stop sending screen output to the file M:RPEDOPS.

7 Finally, to see the results of what you have done, key-in: **TYPE M:RPEDOPS [NO PAGE]{RETURN}** and watch the listing on screen. Remember, 'RPEDOPS' is the file into which you 'PUT' the screen output you generated while using RPED just now.

Note

You can also use the [SYSTEM] option when you PUT printer outputs to file. Here too the PCW will keep direct printer output to a file until you tell it to stop by issuing another PUT command.

Personally, I never use the PUT command – except when I'm writing books about using CP/M – but I work in a very particular way. You too will have your own ways of doing things and, for all I know, PUT may be just the thing you've been looking for. Whether you use it or not is very much up to you.

Automating procedures with GET and SUBMIT

Every so often you will want to carry out routine housekeeping procedures on your discs. For example, you may want to delete all your old .BAK (backup) files from a disc and then convert the remaining master copies into archive files (perhaps with the extension '.ARC'). Then you may want to copy all those archive files onto another safety copy archive disc and keep it separate from the original archive disc. There's no telling what people get up to. You will have to develop your own routines and your own ways of protecting your programs and data.

The fact that such procedures are routine makes them intrinsically boring and often there is no real incentive to carry them out, or worse still, no real incentive to carry them out properly. Wouldn't it be nice then, if you could carry out the whole routine faultlessly by keying in a single command!? Here's how.

I shall have to show you a set of procedures which will work on your system as it is now – you will have to modify things to suit the precise way you work after you have worked through this section.

Note

The procedure we shall be examining works just like the SUBMIT command we saw earlier in this book, so see also the note at the end of this section.

Automating procedures with GET and SUBMIT

1   Start by making sure that your working copy of the CP/M start-up disc is in drive A:. **RESET** or **REBOOT** the system (**SHIFT+EXTRA** then tap **EXIT**).

If we want the computer to carry out a series of tasks, we shall have to give it a series of commands. And, as we shall want to execute the same sequence of commands each time we run our housekeeping routine, it is best to put those commands into an ASCII text file. That way you only have to key them in once and you won't miss any of them out when you come to do your housekeeping at the end of a busy week. Once again we can use RPED.

2   Key-in: **RPED{RETURN}** and when you get its opening display, tap **f4/f3** to create a new file. Put a data disc in drive A: to replace your start-up disc, then key-in the filename, **ROUTINE.SUB{RETURN}** to get RPED's work page.

Note

I have asked you to call this file ROUTINE.SUB, only so we can use it with both the GET and the SUBMIT commands. For the GET command you can call the file pretty well anything you like.

Now I want you to create a file which has the command lines shown on the next page.

Automating procedures with GET and SUBMIT

These command lines will give us our (nonsense) routine – yours will be much more real. The items in brackets are merely my comments on what is happening. Key-in only the items shown **LIKE THIS**.

       M: (log to drive M:)
       DIR [FULL] (get a full directory of drive M:)
       REN SUBMIT.BAK=SUBMIT.COM (rename a .COM file)
       DIR [FULL] (check that REN has worked)
       ERA SUBMIT.BAK (erase the .BAK file on M:)
       PIP M:=A:DATE.COM
       DATE
       A: (log to drive a:)

3   Next tap **EXIT twice** to leave RPED.

4   Before we go any further, let's put a copy of our new file onto the memory drive, key-in: **PIP M:=A:ROUTINE.SUB** and **{RETURN}** it.

5   Now, **if you have one of the original 8000 series machines** replace the data disc in drive A: with your **Programming Utilities disc 3**, otherwise replace the data disc with your working copy of the CP/M start-up disc.

Automating procedures with GET and SUBMIT

So we have finished step one, we have created a permanent record of the commands in our routine procedure. We shall start by using the GET command to implement it.

1   Key-in: **GET CONSOLE INPUT FROM FILE M:ROUTINE.SUB [SYS]**, check what you have keyed-in and if it is correct, keep an eye on the screen and tap the {RETURN} key.

You will see the PCW step through the procedure following each command in turn. At the end you will see how long it is since you started working through this procedure – i.e. after resetting your system at the start.

That's how you use GET to work through a detailed procedure, but as the title of this section tells you, you can use SUBMIT to do the same job. That is why I got you to create a .SUB file to hold the commands. Try this,

1   If you have an 8000 series PCW, put your start-up CP/M disc in drive A:. Then, whatever machine you have, key-in: **SUBMIT M:ROUTINE {RETURN}** and watch the screen again. You will get an error message if your machine is an 8000 series, but it doesn't matter now

Automating procedures with GET and SUBMIT

You will see the PCW implement precisely the same set of commands as it did just now and you can still check how long it took you to do it.

Note

So here again, like PIP and PUT, we have two command programs, GET and SUBMIT which seem at first glance to do the same basic job. But that is due to the example we have seen.

Of these two, SUBMIT is the less cumbersome to use for the purpose we had in mind, but that is offset by the fact that GET has wider uses – particularly if you write your own programs. And in any case we shall be looking at a way to generate quite lengthy command lines with a single stroke of a function key, so it will take the same amount of effort on your part to give either command.

Once again it all boils down to the fact that, if and how you use GET and SUBMIT, depends on you, and the way you work. You have seen the essential principles, but I suspect you will need to experiment with the command programs to get the best out of them.

Tweaking the screen

You have two command programs which enable you to change the way the screen looks. They don't produce spectacular results and they are very easy to use, so we can look at both of them under the same heading. The two command programs in question are 'PALETTE.COM' and 'SET24X80.COM' and they should both be on your CP/M start-up disc. It is easier to demonstrate than to describe what the programs do, so:

PALETTE.COM

1   Put the working copy of your CP/M start-up disc in drive A: and then simply key-in: **PALETTE 1 0** (i.e. the number one and the number zero) and tap **{RETURN}**.

This sets reverse video on for the whole screen – black characters on a light background. On my screens this looks like a recipe for migraine, so I'm going to switch back to normal video!

2   Tap the **COPY** key to recall the last command (incidentally you could also use the PASTE key or ALT-W to do the same job). Delete backwards to get rid of the two numbers, then key-in: **0** (i.e. zero) and **1**, then tap **{RETURN}** to go back to light characters on a dark background which is much less painful.

So 'PALETTE 1 0' sets reverse video on and 'PALETTE 0 1' reverts to normal video.

Tweaking the screen

SET24X80

Your normal PCW screen is 90 characters wide and 31 lines deep, which is fine for most programs, but some require that the screen be the more normal 80 characters by 24 lines. This command enables you to set the screen appropriately.

1 Put the working copy of your CP/M start-up disc in drive A: and then simply key-in: **SET24X80** (all one word!). Keep a close eye on the screen and tap **{RETURN}**.

Nothing very interesting seems to happen, but now try this:

2 Tap the **COPY** key (or PASTE or ^W), tap the **SPACEBAR** and key-in: the word **OFF**. Now put your left forefinger on the **A>** prompt on the screen, to mark its position. Next, watch the **A>** prompt and tap **{RETURN}**.

You will see the A> prompt move up a line when you tap {RETURN} and then you will see it jump up and left as the command takes effect.

The keyboard under CP/M Plus

Throughout this book I have been asking you to key-in certain letters as well as tapping single keys or combinations of keys which do certain specific jobs. It is about time that we drew all these things together and had a more intensive look at the keyboard.

We very much take for granted that when we press a certain key on the keyboard it generates a particular output on screen. Now that might be something simple, like tapping the 'W' key and seeing the letter 'w' appear on the screen, or it might be more complex, like tapping ALT-W and seeing the last command you keyed-in repeated. How does the computer know that the letter 'W' key is the letter 'w'?

When you tap that key, all it knows for certain is that you have tapped the key which is second from the left in the top row of letter keys on the main part of the keyboard. Once it recognises that you have tapped that key on its own, it goes away, generates a letter 'w' and displays it on screen. Why? Because that's what it has been told to do.

In essence this is easy enough to do; you simply give each key a number and then you tell the PCW that a particular key number is equal to a particular character or string of characters. On the PCW 'the key which is second from the left in the top row of letter keys on the main part of the keyboard', is key number 59. So, somewhere in the PCW's memory, is a list which tells it the assignment of every key on the keyboard – including one bit of information which tells it 'key number 59 = "w"'. But it also tells it that key number 59 + either one of the two keys numbered 21 = "W"'.

The keyboard under CP/M Plus

In your PCW User Guide, near the start of the section which describes how to redefine your keyboard, you will find a diagram which gives you the number of each key on the keyboard. We shall need this shortly, because we shall be redefining some of the keys to make them do different jobs. For the moment though, let us have a closer look at the standard keyboard settings. Just in case you haven't yet explored all its capabilities. Here's my chance to be a Smart Alec and show you some useful symbols. Did you know:

If you tap	you get
ALT+9	æ
SHIFT+ALT+9	Æ
EXTRA+C	©
EXTRA+R	®
EXTRA+T	™
SHIFT+ALT+.	●
EXTRA+=	≠
ALT+=	≅
SHIFT+ALT+=	≡

Actually, I'm not really that much of a know-all, because if you look in your User Guide, in the section on CP/M Plus character sets, you will find a table which lists what all the key combinations do on your keyboard. It is well worth a careful look. All I've done here is pick out how you can generate some of the more common symbols; to demonstrate the versatility of your keyboard.

The keyboard - using the NumLock function

There is one key combination which should be given more prominence in the User Guide, the NumLock (and unlock) code. To implement the 'NumLock' function, hold down the **ALT** key and then tap the **RELAY** key.

Tapping these keys brings the number pad into action – i.e. it disables the cursor control arrow keys and enables you to use the pad of number keys to generate numbers. If you decide you want to use the cursor control arrow keys again, you simply tap **ALT+RELAY** again to reinstate them.

So if you are working with an accounts program or a spreadsheet, you can speed up the data entry process by tapping **ALT+RELAY** and then keying-in the numbers on the number pad, rather than using the number keys along the top of the keyboard. On most software you should still be able to move the cursor, but you will have to do it with 'ALT codes' or 'CONTROL codes'. Try this:

1 At the **A>** prompt, key-in: **Now is the time**, then tap the **SPACEBAR**. Now tap-in **ALT-RELAY** to set NumLock on. Now use the number pad to key-in the numbers **1234567890**. Don't tap {RETURN}.

What I want to do now is show you how you can edit this spurious command line, even though the arrow keys no longer work. You can edit any command line provided you haven't tapped {RETURN}.

The keyboard - using the NumLock function

Remember, our cursor control arrow keys have been disabled. What I want you to do is to move back along the pretend command line to the word 'time' and change it to 'hour'.

1 Hold down the **ALT** key and tap the letter **A** repeatedly until the cursor ends up on the 't' of **'time'**. Now tap the DEL→ key four times to delete the word. Next, key-in the word **hour**.

2 Hold down the **ALT** key again and this time tap the letter **F** to move the cursor to the right. Position the cursor on the number '**4**'. Tap the ←**DEL** key once to delete the number **3**, then use the DEL→ key to delete all the remaining numbers, except for the **0** at the end.

3 Finish off the edit by tapping the full stop key, then tapping **0** again. Your pretend command line should now read, '**Now is the hour 12.00**'. Tap {**RETURN**} to get one of CP/M's helpful error messages: '**NOW?**'.

So, ALT-A (or CONTROL-A, or ^A) moves the cursor to the left while ALT-F (or CONTROL-F, or ^F) moves the cursor to the right. (WordStar and SuperCalc users will find these codes familiar.) You won't need to move the cursor up or down while you are editing command lines. Don't forget to cancel the NumLock setting!

The keyboard - ALT or CONTROL codes

The PCW uses several control codes (or ALT codes) which in themselves issue commands to CP/M – they 'control' its actions. The control key (the ALT key on the PCW) works like a special shift key – you might find it referred to as a 'super shift key' in some of the more excitable publications. When you hold down the control or ALT key on a CP/M machine it converts the output from any key you tap at the same time. So, as we saw a short while ago, ALT+W means 'repeat the last command', rather than just the plain 'w' of the W key on its own.

On the PCW, the SHIFT, ALT and EXTRA keys have this feature of amending (shifting) the output from other keys, rather than generating any output of their own. Tap ALT on its own as many times as you like and nothing will happen! So what are the control codes under CP/M and what do they do? And can you generate the same codes by tapping any other keys?

On the next page I have prepared a chart which is designed to answer these questions. The chart does not itemise every control code you can use when you are working with CP/M, but it does list the ones you are most likely to find useful.

Note

Many of the commercial programs you might run on your system use their own system of control codes. There is no guarantee that the codes they use will be the same as those on the chart overleaf.

The keyboard - control codes summary

Control Code (ALT + a letter key)	What it does	Other keys you can use
^A	move cursor left	← ARROW
^B	move cursor to end of command line	SHIFT and SHIFT+EOL
^C	halt operation of a program	STOP
^E	move the cursor down and continue command	ALT+↓ ARROW
^F	move cursor right	→ ARROW or CHAR
^G	delete right	DEL→
^H	delete left	←DEL or CAN
^I	tab (8 spaces)	TAB
^J and ^M	implement a command	{RETURN} or ENTER
^P	printer channel open and close	f7 or f8
^Q	continue suspended screen display	f3 or f4
^R	repeat a line on screen	RELAY
^S	suspend display of information on screen	f5 or f6
^U	abandon the command line being keyed-in	CUT
^W	repeat last command	COPY and PASTE
^X	delete the command you have keyed-in	ALT+←DEL
^Z	end of file marker	f1 or f2

Tweaking the keyboard

During the last few pages we have seen three important points which have a bearing on what we are going to do next:

- Every key on the keyboard is identified by a number (remember, we saw that the key which generates the output, 'w' is key number 59)

- When you start-up your system, CP/M assigns a task to every key on the keyboard and those settings are stored in memory

- You can change the setting for any key, or combination of a key plus one or more 'special shift' keys (SHIFT, ALT or EXTRA).

Redefining the keyboard is a two stage process. You start by creating an ASCII text file which lists the key numbers and the new settings for the keys you want to change – you do not have to key-in a setting for every key on the keyboard! Think of this ASCII file as a 'key definition file' (KDF). In the second stage, you use the CP/M command program SETKEYS.COM to make the changes you have specified in the KDF.

Note

You can have as many KDFs as you like, provided they all have different names. Which means that you can have as many different keyboard settings as you like. But note that you cannot change the key settings under LocoScript.

Tweaking the keyboard - the key definition file

1   Start-up your system with your CP/M start-up disc. When you get the **A>** prompt, key-in: **RPED {RETURN}** and wait for RPED's opening screen. When it appears, replace your start-up disc with a data disc.

2   Tap **f3/f4** to create a new file. Give this file the name **SBSKEYS1** (short for, 'Step-By-Step keys number 1') and confirm it by tapping **{RETURN}**.

For this first file we shall make a simple change, just to illustrate the procedure. We will set things up so the key combination 'ALT+D' gets you a directory of the drive you are logged-to (i.e. the 'active' or 'default' drive). If you look at your keyboard diagram in the PCW User Guide (in Appendix 1, which describes the CP/M Plus character sets and how you redefine the keyboard), you will see that the 'D' key is key number 61. N.B. to get the '↑' symbol on the PCW, tap **EXTRA+U** (or **EXTRA+;**).

3   Key-in the following lines, I shall dissect them for you in a moment. Key-in: **E 155 "DIR↑M"**, then tap **{RETURN}** to move to the next line. Now key-in: **61 A "↑'155'"** and then check that you have keyed-in the lines exactly as I have.

Note
The single and double quote marks are important here!

130

Tweaking the keyboard - the key definition file

The contents of your key definition file should look like this:

E 155 "DIR↑M"
61 A "↑'155'"

So what does all that gibberish mean? We'll look at each line in turn.

Line one, E 155 "DIR↑M"
The 'E' at the start of the line tells CP/M that what follows is an 'Expansion Token'. So what's an Expansion Token!?

If you want a single key to represent more than one character you have to tell CP/M that you are 'expanding' the code which is generated by the key in question. In effect you have to define a label which will be attached to a key and you have to give that label a number. The way you use the expansion token is akin to saying, 'attach label number "n" to key number "nn"'.

The number '155' in our line is the number of the label and the items within the double quote marks comprise the label itself. You know that 'DIR' is the directory command and the '↑M"' which follows is the CP/M code for the {RETURN} key. But why did I choose the number 155? Expansion tokens have to have a number somewhere between 128 and 158 (or #80 and #9E in hexadecimal numbering). By my reckoning, the normal CP/M keyboard set-up uses token numbers 128 to 154 (#80 to #9A), which I don't want to change now, so I used the next available unused number – 155 or #9B).

Tweaking the keyboard - the key definition file

Line two, 61 A "↑'155'"

The number 61 at the start of this line is the number of the 'D' key on the PCW keyboard. The letter 'A' which follows is the 'Shift State' – 'A' represents the ALT key, 'E' represents the EXTRA key, 'S' represents the normal SHIFT keys and 'SA' represents SHIFT+ALT. You can specify, no shift state, or 'normal' shift state with the letter 'N'. You can also specify more than one shift state if you want to. If you do this, the key in question will generate the same result in each shift state you specify.

The items within double and single quotes are the reference to the expansion token you want attached to the key combination ALT and key number 61 – i.e. this line says 'ALT+D = label 155, which = DIR ↑M'.

Note

The lines which set up the expansion tokens and the lines which assign those tokens to particular keys (or key combinations) can be in any order in the key definition file.

4   If you are happy that you have keyed-in the lines correctly, tap **EXIT twice** to leave RPED.

RPED will create our key definition file which we have called SBSKEYS1. But the file by itself is useless. We have to use another CP/M command file to implement it.

Tweaking the keyboard - using the key definition file

The command file we want is on your CP/M start-up disc, but the key definition file is on your data disc, so to make things easier – especially if you have just one floppy disc drive – we had better copy the key definition file onto the memory drive before we go on.

1 Key-in: **PIP M:=A:SBSKEYS1{RETURN}**.

When you get the A> prompt back, we can implement the change to our keyboard. When you are ready:

1 Replace your data disc in drive A: with your CP/M start-up disc. Then key-in: **SETKEYS M:SBSKEYS1{RETURN}**.

Once again, nothing very spectacular seems to happen, but when you get the A> prompt back once more:

2 Tap **ALT-D** and watch the screen. You will get a directory of drive A:. Now key-in **M:{RETURN}**, then **ALT-D** and watch the screen. This time you get a directory of drive M:, because it is now the active, or default, drive – the one you are logged to. Log back to drive A: with **A:{RETURN}**.

I want to go on now and build a key definition file which you might find useful in future. We'll set up a number of keys so they'll do fairly common jobs – the sort of things you will want to do frequently when you are working with CP/M.

133

Tweaking the keyboard to streamline your work

1 With your CP/M start-up disc in drive A:, key-in: **RPED {RETURN}** and wait for RPED's opening screen. Then, replace the start-up disc in drive A: with the data disc which holds the file 'SBSKEYS1'. Tap **f1/f2** to edit an existing file and then key-in the file name **SBSKEYS1** and tap **{RETURN}**. For the 'destination' file name, key-in: **MYKEYS**, delete the remainder of the offered name and tap **{RETURN}**.

Before we go any further, let's just have a look at the elements of the task we are about to undertake.

- I want us to set up some of your keys so you can work more easily and efficiently

- Your keyboard already has function keys – i.e. keys designed to perform a task or a function, rather than merely generate letters or numbers – so it seems sensible that we extend their capabilities

- We can do that and still leave the normal settings intact by using the ALT key with the function keys to generate the end result we want

- Under the normal keyboard set-up we have four expansion tokens which are unused (155 to 158). So, if we want to create more than four new tasks we shall have to replace some of the existing expansion tokens

Tweaking the keyboard to streamline your work

- Replacing the existing expansion tokens will alter the way some of the keys behave. So we need to be careful about how we select the expansion tokens to replace

- We can find out the numbers of the 'f' keys by looking at the diagram in your PCW User Guide (in the section which describes how you set up a key definition file – KDF).

Once we have these points clear in our minds we can begin the job of setting up our new KDF. I suggest that we assign tasks, or functions, to keys as follows:

KEY		WHAT IT WILL GENERATE
02	f1	DIR [SIZE]↑ M
02 shifted	f2	DIR M: [SIZE]↑ M
00	f3	PIP↑ M
00 shifted	f4	REN↑ M
73	f5	TYPE
73 shifted	f6	ERA
77	f7	RPED↑ M
77 shifted	f8	DISCKIT↑ M

You can change these settings later if they don't suit you.

Tweaking the keyboard to streamline your work

Remember, we have RPED running and we are ready to create our KDF. We shall start by amending the first line of our existing file.

2 Move the cursor across so it is on the upward pointing arrow after the word 'DIR'. Now tap the **SPACEBAR** once and then key-in: **[SIZE]**. Next, to move down a line, tap the cursor control ↓ **ARROW**. Then tap the **CUT** key to delete the line.

3 Move the cursor to the left margin and key-in:
E 156 "DIR M: [SIZE]↑ M" (remember, you generate the upward pointing arrow '↑' by tapping EXTRA+U). Finish the line by tapping **{RETURN}**.

4 Now key-in the following lines:
E 157 "PIP↑ M"
E 158 "REN ↑ M"
E 130 "TYPE "   (N.B. Followed by a space)
E 132 "ERA "   (N.B. Followed by a space)
E 134 "RPED↑ M"
E 136 "DISCKIT↑ M"   and tap {RETURN}

I have chosen to use the expansion tokens numbered 130, 132, 134 and 136 because they are duplicates – i.e. where a function key returns the same code, either shifted or unshifted – when we have finished this section, they will return the code only when unshifted.

136

Tweaking the keyboard to streamline your work

At this stage we have merely defined our new expansion tokens. We have to go on now and assign those tokens to particular keys.

1 Tap **{RETURN}** once more to skip a line in our file (purely for tidiness).

2 Now key-in the following lines. Notice the format as you do so.
   02 A "↑'155'"   (N.B. 'A' = ALT)
   02 SA "↑'156'"   (N.B. 'SA' = SHIFT+ALT)

   00 A "↑'157'"
   00 SA "↑'158'"

   73 A "↑'130'"
   73 SA "↑'132'"

   77 A "↑'134'"
   77 SA "↑'136'"

3 Now tap the **EXIT** key **twice** to leave RPED.

4 We can speed things up by putting a copy of the KDF on the memory drive and then copying it to our start-up disc. So key-in: **PIP M:=A:MYKEYS {RETURN}**. Then put your start-up disc in drive A: and key-in: **PIP A:=M:MYKEYS** followed by **{RETURN}**.

137

Tweaking the keyboard to streamline your work

Now to implement our new function key settings. We shall start by resetting the keyboard to its normal functions.

1 With your CP/M start-up disc in drive A: reset the system with **SHIFT+EXTRA** and **EXIT**.

2 Now we shall try out our new keyboard definition file. Key-in: **SETKEYS MYKEYS {RETURN}**.

If you have keyed-in the lines exactly as they are printed in this book, nothing much should seem to happen. There will be a short pause and then the A> prompt will return to the screen. If you get an error message, it means that there is a problem with your key definition file and you will need to use RPED to check and amend any mistakes you made. Then you will need to put the amended copy of the KDF on your CP/M start-up disc as we did on the previous page. Only then can you restart this page.

Now to see if our KDF worked.

1 Tap **ALT-f1/f2** and you should get a directory of drive A: (the logged drive). Hold down a **SHIFT** key and tap **ALT-f1/f2** (i.e. 'ALT-f2') and you will get a directory of drive M:. Try out all of your new ALT + function key settings.

Loading your new keyboard settings automatically

Your new keyboard settings provide you with some useful timesavers, so you might want to load the settings automatically when you start-up your system. Here's how.

1   Tap **f7** to start up RPED.

You see, it's saving us time already!.

2   Tap **f1** to edit an existing file and then key-in: **PROFILE.SUB** and tap **{RETURN}**. Tap **{RETURN}** again so RPED will save the amended file under the same name as the original file.

3   Move your cursor down one line, so it is on the first 'P' of PIP. Then hold down the **ALT** key and tap the ↓ **ARROW** to insert a new line. Now key-in: **SETKEYS MYKEYS**.

Note

If you have a 9000 series machine you will probably find that PROFILE.SUB does not automatically copy ERASE.COM and TYPE.COM into memory. You need these programs if your new function key settings are to work all the time, so, while you are at it, you might also like to insert a couple of lines into the PIP commands so they are loaded when you start up.

Loading your new keyboard settings automatically

4   Finally, tap **EXIT twice** to leave RPED.

Now, each time you start up your system, it will automatically implement the keyboard settings you have defined.

1   To check this out, reset the PCW now with **SHIFT+EXTRA** and **EXIT**. Watch the screen as you do so and you will see your new command(s) take effect.

2   Now try out the ALT+function key settings again.

A final word or two

I never thought that writing a book about CP/M would be interesting, but I was wrong. I hope it has been interesting to read, too.

CP/M is one of those things that is there all the time, but you don't really take any notice of. I have a feeling that, even experienced users of CP/M, rarely exploit more than about 20 percent of its features. Now whether this is because we are lazy or because we just don't have the time to experiment, I wouldn't like to say.

Of course, there is no guarantee that everybody uses the same 20 percent. And, as I've tried to intimate throughout this book, we all have our own ways of working. So I suppose the point of a book like this one is, to try and show, not all, but far more than 20 percent of what it can do so you can make up your own mind as to which 20 percent you are going to use most in the future. You may decide to go far further into CP/M than I have in this book: there are many aspects I have not covered, because they are not within the 20 percent that we, average, users tend to employ. If you decide to go in for machine code programming, for example, then you will want to look at a range of other 'programming utilities' which come with CP/M Plus.

But I hope the book has made you aware that CP/M Plus – for all its brusque unfriendliness – is a useful tool. It's a bit like having a mate you can rely on, who just gets on with the job and doesn't say much. Once you can come to terms with someone like that they are easy enough to live with. The same goes for CP/M. Once you've got the hang of it – once you know how it needs to be treated and talked to – then it all becomes easy. So good luck with it in the future.

Appendix A
Using Other Printers

Why use other printers?

I suspect that the 'typical' PCW user will be quite happy to work with the printer which comes with their machine. But, just in case you have LocoScript 2 on the 8000 series, or you write your own programs, and you fancy using another printer, I want to discuss some of the things you will have to bear in mind.

Firstly, why might you want to use another printer?

There would seem to be two main possibilities: One, you might want a faster printer, or two, you might want access to a wider range of type faces and 'print enhancement' options.

So what types of printer are available?

For typical word processing work there are three main types: The 'Daisy Wheel Printer', the 'Laser Printer' and the 'Dot Matrix Printer'. There are other types of printers, such as Ink Jet, Thimble, Line, but at the time of writing these are less widely used than the three main ones I have mentioned.

What are the differences between the three main types of printer?

The daisy wheel printer has at its 'business end' a print wheel which has letters at the end of thin flat 'spokes' which radiate from the centre of the wheel like daisy petals (hence the name 'daisy wheel'). The printer prints a letter on the paper by moving the appropriate petal into the right position and then striking the back of the petal with a print 'hammer'.

Why use other printers?

The letter moves forward against the ribbon and then against the paper, so producing a letter on the page, in essence the printing method is the same as an ordinary typewriter. You get different styles of print by changing the print wheel - each type of print wheel having a different type face and that's something you can't do with an ordinary typewriter.

The dot matrix printer prints in a different way. Instead of having a fixed selection of characters ranged around a wheel which are then struck by a single hammer, the print head itself is formed of a bundle of thin rods which can all be moved independently.

In effect, each rod works like a print hammer which strikes the ribbon, creating a printed dot on the paper. When several rods move forward at the same time they create a pattern of dots on the paper - and if you move the right pattern of rods forward at the same time, they create the shape of a letter.

A laser printer prints in a very similar way to a photocopier, in that it creates an electrostatic image on a revolving drum. This image attracts a layer of 'toner' powder which is then transferred to the paper and fused in position, thus creating the printed page. The letters it produces are made up of dots, like a dot matrix printer, but many more of them. On an average laser printer there will be 300 dots per inch, though some have only 150 dpi. At the top end of the scale (if you can afford it) you can get 1200 dpi.

Why use other printers?

Why would you use one type of printer rather than another?

A daisy wheel printer generally produces much better quality print, than a dot matrix. The image is crisp and clean because the shapes of the characters are formed by continuous lines and curves. In fact daisy wheel output is often referred to as letter quality printing.

But the printing mechanism has to work very hard to achieve high printing speeds. A rating of 50 characters per second (50 cps) is a good one for a daisy wheel printer. But speed ratings can be misleading. Often the speed rating given for a printer is actually its maximum speed. A printer with a maximum speed of 50 cps is likely to have an average printing speed of somewhere between 30 and 40 cps.

A laser printer also produces a very high quality result. Even at 300 dots per inch it is difficult for the average person to spot that the letters are not made up of lines and curves. But at 1200 dots per inch it delivers typesetting quality output. A laser printer usually gives you a wide range of typefaces and type styles, as well as a graphics capability. They are also very fast. The one drawback is, they are expensive, but prices are coming down.

Generally speaking, because the dot matrix printer forms the outline of a character with dots rather than lines and curves, the quality of output cannot be as crisp and clean as the daisy wheel (that's why the best output is called near letter quality rather than letter quality).

Why use other printers?

Where speed is concerned, the picture is more complicated. As we have seen, a daisywheel printer is quite slow when compared with the other two main types: a dot matrix printer in drafting mode might well print at 350 cps plus. And even in 'NLQ' mode, speeds of 80 cps are quite common. And, because laser printers print a whole page in one go, (my fairly typical one produces a page every 15 seconds or so), they are faster still. (The 'official' figures for my printer state that it prints at 6 pages per minute, but that, I suspect, doe not allow time for loading its fonts and for closing down after it has finished printing.)

Note

We can make a totally spurious calculation – something an apprentice advertising executive might do – as follows: 'If we say that the average A4 page of typing has something like 60 lines of text, each line being 65 characters wide, then we end up with a total of 3900 characters per page. And if we further say that the laser printer takes 15 seconds to produce a page, then this equates to a print speed of 260 cpi at very best quality of output.'

If and when you do decide to use another printer with your PCW, you need to remember some key points. You will realise that it has to be instructed to stop using one printer and to use another one instead. But there is more to it than that - as you will see on the next couple of pages.

Before the PCW can carry out your instruction to use another printer it has to 'know' certain things about how it should use the new printer.

Using other printers - some key points

The PCW 'talks' to the printer by transmitting characters and control codes along a printer cable. But it can send that information 'down the line' in two ways: Either as a steady stream of characters, one after the other, like a ribbon of electrical signals, or it can chop up the stream of signals into regular lengths of, say, 8 units and then transmit them 8 at a time. The first method is known as 'serial transmission', the second, as 'parallel transmission'.

Both the printer and the PCW must be set up to work in one or other of these modes - in other words they must both be set up to work either via a 'serial interface' or via a 'parallel interface'. The key point here is that the two methods of transmission are quite different - they require different types of cables and they require different kinds of plugs, so your computer must know which plug socket to use when it talks to the printer.

Your computer probably has two printer sockets (or printer ports): One for the standard PCW printer (the round one) and a parallel port which conforms to the 'Centronics' standard. But if you have one of the original 8000 series machines you will have only one 'printer output port' – the one which the dot matrix printer fits into. However, both the 8000 and 9000 machines have another 'expansion' port, to which you can fit (among other things) a 'Serial Input Output and/or Centronics' adapter, so I shall assume, for the moment that you have decided to use the expansion port to connect to your other printer. (If you have a 9000 series machine and you want to use a modem then you will need the adapter for its serial output.)

Using other printers - fitting an adapter

As I write this book the latest 9000 series machines have the expansion port in a position which makes it difficult to use the existing 'SIO/Centronics' adapters, but I dare say this will have changed by the time you read these words.

So, for the purposes of these pages, I shall assume that you have decided to use another printer and that you have bought the appropriate SIO/Centronics adapter for your machine.

Fitting the adapter to your machine is very simple.

1 Start by making sure your machine is switched off. Next, check that the adapter is the right way up (on the 9512 the printer output sockets point upwards, on the 8000 series machines they point to the outside edge of the machine).

2 Then (gently but firmly) push the adapter onto the edge connecter that sticks through the casing of the machine and do up the two screws that are supplied with the kit.

3 Now switch on your machine and start up with your normal start-up disc.

Everything will seem to work exactly as before, but if you look closely at the CP/M sign-on message at the top of the screen, you will see that it has changed.

Telling the PCW to use another printer

CP/M has recognised the fact that the 'SIO/Centronics add-on' has been fitted. But that is all that has changed. If you try to print something it will still use the built-in printer and it will do so until you tell it to do otherwise. So how do you tell it to use your other printer? Here again I have to make an assumption. I shall assume that your other printer – not the one that came with the machine – is a fairly standard dot matrix printer.

Note

I chose to use the 'Serial Input Output and/or Centronics' adapter for my system because the Centronics interface uses standard plugs and cables, and a standard way of transmitting information down the line. There are actually two types of standard Centronics plug: male and female. You will probably need a cable which, like mine, has a male plug at each end.

1 Remove the disc from the drive and switch off the PCW. Make sure the printer is also switched off. Connect the printer to the PCW via the standard Centronics cable. Then switch on the printer and start-up the PCW again.

Now we need to tell CP/M to use your other printer, using the command program DEVICE.COM. If you have an 8000 series machine, this program is on your Programming Utilities disc, disc 3, so have a working copy of this disc to hand.

Telling the PCW to use another printer

1 Start up your machine in the normal way and (if you have an 8000 series machine, put the working copy of disc 3 in drive A:) then key-in: **DEVICE LST: = CEN {RETURN}**.

2 Now let's see if it worked. Put some paper in your other printer, then tap **ALT-P** followed by **ALT-f1/f2**.

You should hear the printer print out a copy of the directory for drive A:. This shows us that CP/M is directing printer output to the Centronics port.

3 Tap ALT-P again to close the printer channel.

If you have a 9000 series machine and you want to use the built-in parallel port you will need to see your dealer to get a special cable which fits the PCW at one end and the printer at the other. Once you have this all connected up, you issue a slightly different DEVICE command: i.e. instead of keying-in DEVICE LST: = CEN {RETURN} as we did in step 1 above, you would key-in: DEVICE LST: = PAR {RETURN}. This instructs the PCW to send printer output to the built-in parallel port on the machine instead of to the PCW's own printer.

You may decide that you want to create a start-up disc which automatically activates the Centronics or the parallel port during the start-up process. If this is so, you will need to put another command in your PROFILE.SUB file.

Setting up another printer automatically

1 Start-up the machine in the normal way, then tap **ALT-f7/f8** to run RPED. Load the PROFILE.SUB file and add the line: **DEVICE LST: = CEN** (or **DEVICE LST: = PAR** if you are going to use the built-in parallel port on a 9000 series machine). Then save the file.

Note

If you have an 8000 series machine you will have to do some housekeeping for this new command to work. The command program DEVICE.COM is on disc 3, but you will need a copy of it on your start-up disc. Now, if your start-up disc is a straight copy of the CP/M Plus disc 2 then you will not have enough room left on the disc. So you will need to make some room by erasing some of the files you are unlikely to use. For example, the average user is unlikely to want to use the files 'ED.COM, LANGUAGE.COM, PALETTE.COM, PAPER.COM, SET24X80.COM'. So I would be tempted to get rid of them from my copy disc. That will leave plenty of room for DEVICE.COM.

Then it is simply a matter of PIPping a copy of the file from disc 3 onto the memory drive and then PIPping a copy from the memory drive onto your copy start-up disc.

Thereafter, each time you start up with this disc, the PCW will automatically direct printer output to your newly defined printer port.

Setting up a serial input/output

Once you have your SIO/Centronics add-on you can use it either for a centronics printer or as a serial interface. The serial interface will drive either a printer or some other 'serial device', such as a modem, that will enable you to interact with other computers down a telephone line. But before you can use the serial interface you will have to set it up with a program called SETSIO.COM which is on your CP/M start-up disc.

You will find an explanation of how to use this command program in the CP/M section of your PCW User Guide. It will also cross refer you to associated topics in the Guide.

I do not want to go into the detail of the jargon you will find in the description, because the RS232C serial interface deserves at least a decent chapter of a book in its own right. Suffice it to say that if you buy a modem, or a printer, or any other piece of equipment that uses the serial interface, the documentation you get with the equipment will give you full details of how you should set-up your PCW serial input/output port. The description in the User Guide will then tell you how to implement the correct settings.

Here too, it may be sensible to implement the commands automatically during the start-up procedure, via PROFILE.SUB.

Appendix B
Glossary

Glossary

In the main body of the book I have tried to define jargon words as they arose. This appendix takes that process a little further by gathering together a few more definitions for some of the jargon surrounding word processing and computers in general.

ALT Key
A key which works like a 'super' shift key. It enables the PCW keyboard to generate ALTernative results using the various keys on the keyboard. It performs the same function as the 'Control' key on other computers.

Ambiguous (file names)
With CP/M you can key in commands which include file names incorporating 'wild-card' characters - i.e. characters which represent another character - thus creating a file name ('mask') which can apply to more than one file. In this sense such file names are ambiguous.

Artwork
Finished graphics and text ready for the 'page-make-up' or duplication stages of the print process.

ASCII
A standard computer industry code for representing letters, numbers, symbols etc. - American Standard Code for Information Interchange.

Ascender
That part of a lower case letter which ascends above the normal letter height (example, the letter 'h' has an ascender).

157

Glossary

Aspect Ratio
The relative proportions (length of sides to length of top and bottom) of a piece of artwork.

Back-up
(verb) The process of creating duplicate copies of files or discs.
(noun) A duplicate - safety copy of a file or disc.

Baseline
A theoretical line on which the letters in a typeface stand.

Bleed
The space on a page between the text area and the edges of the page.

Body Copy
All text on a page other than headings, sub-heads, captions, etc..

Body Type
The typeface used for body copy.

Booting
The start-up procedure for a computer system, during which the computer 'reads-in' the operating system from disc.

Bullet
A large dot or other symbol used to highlight and mark the beginning of an item in a list.

Glossary

Camera Ready
Completed artwork which is ready for the next (photographic) stage of the print production process.

Command
An instruction (or a set of instructions) keyed in at the keyboard, telling the computer to carry out a particular job.

COM
The file name extension used for a 'command file' - a computer program written in the computer's internal language.

Copy
(verb) To make a duplicate version of a file or a disc.
(noun) An impressive way of saying 'text'.

Copyfitting
The process of making text fit into the space available for it.

Cropping
Trimming a photograph or an illustration to make the bit you want to show fit into the space available for it.

Cursor
A marker on your screen, usually a bar or rectangle of light. It is there to tell you where you are working on the screen display.

Glossary

Cursor Keys
A set of keys marked with arrows pointing up, down, left and right. You use these keys to move the cursor around the screen.

Data Disc
A disc on which you store files which you have created by using a computer program, such as RPED or your word processing system.

Data File
A file which holds information.

Default Settings
When you start up a computer system or a software program it has to make certain assumptions about the way you want to work. It has to adopt standard settings for a wide range of things. Thus the program will work in a particular way in 'default' of any instructions to the contrary. In other words it will adopt certain 'default settings'.

Delete or Erase
To rub out or erase items which have put themselves in by mistake.

Descender
The bit of a lower case letter which hangs down below the baseline (as in 'g' or 'j' or 'p').

Disc (or Disk)
A flat circular piece of plastic with a magnetic surface which you use to store 'permanent' copies of data and program files.

Glossary

Disc (or Disk) continued
A 'Floppy Disc' for the PCW is housed in a rigid plastic sleeve which has slots to enable the computer to read the information stored on the disc.

Disc Drive
The part of the computer system which spins the disc in its protective covering while the computer is reading from or writing to it.

Documentation
The manuals supplied with your PC or its software, which are supposed to explain how to use the system.

Dot Matrix Printer
A printer which uses a set of pins to create a pattern of dots on paper. By varying the pattern you create the shapes of the different characters.

DPI
Short for 'Dots Per Inch'. When you produce finished output (with anything other than a daisywheel printer), the quality of that output is measured in DPI. The higher the number of DPI the better the quality of the output.

Dropped Cap(ital)
Large capital letters are sometimes used for the first letter of a paragraph. Such letters are called 'dropped' caps because the first letter drops down from the top of text instead of standing up above the rest.

Glossary

Editing
The process of amending, inserting or deleting text and layouts.

Em
Technically, an Em is the square of the size of the typeface - so a 36 point Em will measure 36pt by 36pt. In practice, when designers or printers talk about Ems they usually mean a 12pt Em (i.e. a space measuring 12pt by 12pt, or 1/6th of an inch square, or yet again, 1 pica square).

En
A space which is half as wide as an Em.

ENTER Key
The key with which you 'enter' (i.e. confirm) your instructions or selections from menus. The RETURN key performs the same function in most kinds of software, though it can vary.

File
A collection of information stored as a separate entity with its own special filename. You can have data files and program files (i.e. files which hold programs).

File Name Mask
See 'Ambiguous'.

Floppy Disc
A flexible sheet of recording material in the shape of a disc.

Glossary

Font (Fount)
The set of characters which comprise a typeface.

Format
(noun) 1. The layout of a page.
(noun) 2. The method for organising the storage space on a disc.
(verb) To prepare a disc for use on your computer system by laying down a new pattern of magnetic 'tracks' on its surface ready to store information.

Function Keys
A set of keys on your computer keyboard which are pre-programmed to do certain jobs (i.e. to perform certain functions).

Galley
The end result of the typesetting process - a long strip of typeset text ready to be cut and pasted-up.

Gutter
The white space between adjoining columns of text.

Half-tone
A photograph is made up of continuous shades or tones, but the print process cannot reproduce these, so printers break up the initial image into a pattern of dots - the different intensities simulating a continuous gradation of tones. (See also 'Screening'.)

Glossary

Hard Copy
A copy of your work printed out on paper. Also known as a 'printout'.

Hardware
The physical components which make up your computer system, such as the keyboard, disc drive, monitor, printer.

Housekeeping
Those necessary activities which are not concerned directly with using your PCW as a word processing system, but without which, things would soon get in a mess. For example, carrying out routine checks of what information you are holding on a particular disc, erasing unwanted material, renaming files, copying files, etc..

Hyphenation
Fitting lines of text into the space available for it by breaking some words into two and distributing the two sections of the word between the end of one line and the start of the next. The first part of the word (and therefore the line) ends in a hyphen.

Input
(verb) The process of getting information into a computer system.
(noun) Information which has been put in to a computer system.

Justification
The process of lining text up to a margin (also known as 'ranging' the text). The text in this glossary is 'ranged right' as well as 'ranged left'. Text can also be ranged to the centre of the space available.

Glossary

'k' or 'K'
This is short for kilo, or one thousand bytes. Actually there are 1024 bytes in one kilobyte, so in computer terminology '1k' actually means 'near enough a thousand'.

Kerning
The ability of some DTP systems to adjust the space between letters.

Laser Printer
At first glance it looks like a photocopier and, indeed, it works in a very similar way, except, the image is created in the computer rather than by a photographic process.

Layout
The plan for how the final page will look.

Leading
(Pronounced 'ledding') is the space between lines of typeset text - it used to refer to the strips of lead which were used physically to separate lines.

Ligature
Certain groups of letters which look better when 'run together' as a single character (e.g. ffi, ll).

Measure
Printers' term for the width of the line (in picas).

Glossary

Memory The computer's 'internal store' in which it holds programs and data while you are working with them.

Menu
A list displayed by a computer program that tells you which activities are available at a particular point in the program.

Monitor
A high quality screen or 'visual display unit' (VDU) which enables you to see what you are keying in, as you key it in. It also displays the results of the computer's processing activity.

Mouse
A device which enables you to 'input' instructions to the computer by moving a pointer on your screen, (so it points at a picture or a menu), rather than by keying in lengthy sequences of commands.

Operating System
A type of computer program which controls or 'manages' the way the computer and all the other items of hardware operate as a single system.

Orphan
A single word moved onto a new column or page during copyfitting (small relative of a 'widow').

Output
(verb) To transmit information from the computer or some other device.

Glossary

Output continued
(noun) The information you get out of your computer (via the printer, or a disc drive, or on screen).

Overmatter
Bits of text left over after copyfitting.

Overwrite
To write data on top of data which is already stored in the computer's memory, or on disc, and thus replace it.

Page Make-up
The actual process of assembling text, illustrations, headings etc. into the finished page.

Pica
A unit of measurement equal to about 1/6th of an inch.

Point
A unit of measurement equal to 1/12th of a pica - roughly 1/72nd of an inch. (To be very precise, 72 points = 0.996264 ins.)

Printer
(1) The machine attached to the computer which prints out hard copies of the work you have been doing.
(2) The person who will have the printed copies of your report ready on Thursday – just as he did last week.

Glossary

Printer Driver
That part of your computer system which controls the printer.

Prompt
An instruction on the screen telling you what to do next.

Proportional
On a typewriter and on your computer's screen, an 'i' takes up the same amount of space as an 'm'. With proportional spacing, the different sizes of the letters are taken into account when the text is laid out, so an 'i' takes up about half the space of an 'm'.

Quit
To finish doing a particular job with your software, or finish working with the software itself.

Ragged Edge
Text which has only one end of its lines lined up vertically.

RAM
Random Access Memory. That part of the computer's memory which is available for you to use for loading and running programs and for entering and processing data.

Record
A single set of data held in a data file. A data 'file' contains a number of 'records', each one consisting of individual 'fields'.

Glossary

Reformat
(In word processing) to change the layout (i.e. the format) of text, giving it, for example, different margins, page lengths and so on.

Reset
To repeat the start-up or 'Boot' procedure.

Resolution
The number of dots per inch printed by the printer, or the number of elements per inch which make up the image on the computer screen.

ROM
Read-Only Memory. The computer memory in which information is stored permanently and cannot be altered by program instructions.

Rule
Printers' jargon for a straight line.

Scanner
A device for converting images into a form which the computer can manipulate.

Screening
The process by which a photograph (with continuous tones) is converted into a pattern of dots (half tone).

Glossary

Scrolling
The process of moving your screen display up and down or side to side to enable you to get a particular section of the display on screen.

Software
Programs which enable the very stupid hardware to do a useful job.

Text
The words and characters (letters, numbers, spaces and symbols) which make up a finished document.

Tint
A particular density of dots in an image. Different tints produce different shades of grey in a black and white reproduction process.

VDU
See Monitor.

Wild Cards
A character which can be used to represent another character (just like wild cards in poker). Under DOS there are two wild card characters '?' and '*'. The '?' represents any other single character, the '*' represents any group of characters.

Widow
A single line of text which is pushed into the next column or onto the next page during copyfitting (a bigger version of an orphan).

Glossary

Word Processor

A computer driven by a software program that enables you to carry out the tasks of writing, editing and printing all kinds of documents.

Word Wrap

A word processing feature in which the word processor works out where a line of text should end and it then 'wraps' any uncompleted word down to the left hand end of a new line, so you can keep typing without having to worry about when you get to the end of your typing line.

WYSIWYG

'What You See Is What You Get'. A computer text and picture processing feature in which the screen display closely emulates how the finished document will look on the page.

Index

A

ALT code or control code	33
ALT codes	33
ALT codes, summary	127
ALT codes, summary chart	128
ambiguous file names	45
ASCII files	22
automatic procedures with GET and SUBMIT	116

B

booting and rebooting the system	29, 78
booting direct into a program	82, 86

C

carriage return control code	56
clock, checking	110
clock, setting	109
command line	20
command line, components of	20
command	
8000COPY	103
DATE	109
DEVICE	151
DIR	36, 88
DIR (variants)	90
DIRS	93
DISCKIT	80
DISCKIT (copying a disc)	99
ERA	62
ERA confirm option - [C]	63
ERASE or ERA	30

Index

command (continued)
- GET — 116
- HELP — 9
- PALETTE — 121
- PIP — 24, 49
- PIP - creating a file — 95
- PIP enhancements — 54
- PIP verify option - [V] — 73
- PUT — 111
- PUT [SYSTEM] option — 114
- REN — 47
- SET — 26
- SET24X80 — 121
- SETKEYS — 133, 138
- SETSIO — 154
- SHOW — 96
- SHOW (variants) — 98
- SUBMIT — 23, 1 16
- TYPE — 21, 51

commands
- keying-in — 20
- permanent — 17
- repeating the previous — 60, 74, 109
- transient — 17

confirm option the - [C] — 59
control code or ALT code — 33
- ^A — 126
- ^C — 33
- ^F — 126
- ^J (line feed) — 56
- ^M (carriage return) — 56
- ^Q — 53
- ^P — 51
- ^RELAY (NumLock) — 125
- ^S — 53
- ^W — 121
- ^Z (end of file) — 56

Index

control codes, summary	127
control codes, summary chart	128
copying a disc	99
copying a file	24
CP/M, basic components	17
CP/M, function of	3
CP/M, why you need it	14
creating a file with PIP	95
cursor control, ALT/Control codes	126

D

data disc, creating	81
default drive	49, 89
deleting (erasing) a file	62 - 63
device names	54
device, redirecting outputs	111
direct printing from the keyboard	56
directories	88
directory entries, maximum number of	94
disc drive, default	49
disc drives	5
disc drives, setting attributes for	71
DISCKIT, formatting with	80
discs, care of checklist	8, 77
discs,	
checking the available space	96
copying	99
copying with 8000copy	103
creating a data disc	79
formatting	79 - 81
giving them a name	72
logging between	49
displaying the contents of a file	51
drive B: on a single drive machine	90
drives - default drive	49, 89

Index

E

end of file control code	56
ERA command	63
erasing (deleting) a file	62, 63
expansion port	149
expansion tokens	131
expansion tokens - assigning to keys example	137
expansion tokens - examples of	136

F

file name masks	45
file names	43
file names, ambiguous	45
file type extensions, ones to avoid	44
file, displaying the contents of	51
filename masks	45
files	
.SUB - creating procedure	30
ambiguous names	45
care of	77
copying	49
copying contents to the printer	55
copying more than one at a time	54
copying the contents to the screen	54
creating direct from keyboard	57
creating read only files	92
creating system files	92
erasing (deleting)	62, 63
key definition	129
making one by combining others	58
naming rules - ambiguous file names	45
naming rules and storing	43
protecting	64

Index

read only	64
renaming	47
setting passwords	69
setting to RO	92
setting to SYS	92
system files	65, 92
user numbers	67, 95

H

HELP facility	9
housekeeping, typical activities	19

K

key definition file	129
key definition file - suggested	134
keyboard	
activating the number pad	125
expansion tokens	131
expansion tokens - assigning	137
expansion tokens - examples of	136
generating some useful symbols	124
implementing new definitions	138
key definition file	129
key definition file - suggestion	134
key expansion tokens	131
key expansion tokens - numbering	131
NumLock function	125
redefining its operation	129
shift states	132
special symbols	124
under CP/M Plus	123
keying-in a command	20

Index

L

line feed control code	56
listing the contents of a file	51

M

making the PCW do several tasks in one go	116
masks - filenames	45

N

number pad, activating	125
NumLock key combination	125

O

operating system	3

P

passwords - setting up	69
passwords, modes of protection	70
passwords, setting up	70
PIP, creating a file with	95
printer, types	145
printers	
general description	145
using others	145
Centronics parallel interface	149
serial interface	149

Index

setting up another automatically	153
SIO/Centronics adapter - fitting	149
telling the PCW to use another	151
PROFILE.* file	22
PROFILE.SUB	82
PROFILE.SUB, effects of	26
PROFILE.SUB, submitting automatically	29
Protecting files	64

R

read only files	64
rebooting the PCW (example of)	66
rebooting the system	29, 78
redefining keyboard operation	129
redisplaying the previous command	109
renaming a file	47
renaming files	47
repeating the previous command	60, 74, 109, 121
resetting the system	29, 78
resetting the system (example)	66
RPED	
creating a new file	34
deleting a whole line	35
editing an existing file	37
editing controls	87
inserting a blank line	35
using	31
working with	87

S

search path, setting	26
Serial Input Output/Centronics adapter	149

Index

serial input/output - setting up	154
Setting a password	69
shift states	132
submit RPED	86
SUBMIT.COM	82
system files	65

T

TYPE command	21
TYPE command, suspending the listing	53
TYPE, TYPE PROFILE.*	20

U

user number, logging on with	95
user numbers	95

PC PLUS STEP by STEP

This series, designed for clarity and ease of use, is intended for those who wish to get off to a flying start when faced with new software, operating systems or machines. These books take you through, step-by-step, the processes and functions that will enable you to maximise your effectiveness FAST. The books are written by users for users and are now published in association with PC PLUS, the UK's best-selling PC-specific magazine. The Step by Step series and PC PLUS magazine provide the complete package for all IBM - Compatible personal computer users.

WORDPROCESSORS

Using Locoscript PC (Version 1.5)
John Campbell
0 7506 0249 X   £14.95

Using Wordperfect for Windows
Arthur Tennick
0 7506 0359 3   £14.95

Using MS Word 5.0
Roger Carter
0 434 90316 7   £14.95

Using Wordperfect 5.0
Gautier
0 434 90656 5   £14.95

Using Word for Windows
Alan Balfe
0 7506 0205 8   £14.95

Using Wordstar 5, 5.5 & 6
Alan Balfe
0 7506 0341 0   £14.95

SPREADSHEETS

Using Excel 3.0
Roger Carter
0 7506 0360 7   £14.95

Using Lotus 1-2-3 Release 3
Stephen Morris
0 434 91292 1   £14.95

Using Lotus 1-2-3 Macros
Ian Sinclair
0 7506 0198 1   £16.25

Quattro Pro 3
P K McBride
0 7506 0358 5   £14.95

Lotus 1-2-3 for Windows
Arthur Tennick
0 7506 0607 X   £14.95

DATABASES

Paradox 3.5 for Windows
P K McBride
0 7506 0610 X   £14.95

Using Superbase 2 & 4
Arthur Tennick
0 7506 0042 X   £14.95

Using Q & A
Roger Carter
0 4349 0224 1   £14.95

Using dBASE IV
Roger Carter
0 434 90251 9   £14.95

UTILITIES

Using Disk & RAM Utilities
Ian Sinclair
0 434 91892 X   £14.95

OPERATING SYSTEMS

MS—Dos 5.0
Alan Balfe
0 7506 0471 9   £14.95

Using Windows 3
Arthur Tennick
0 7506 0080 2   £14.95

CP/M Plus on the Amstrad PCW
John Cambell
0 7506 0460 3   £14.95

MACHINE GUIDE

Exploiting the Amstrad PCW 9512
John Campbell & Marion Pye
0 7506 0075 6   £14.95

Using the Amstrad PC1512/1640
Second edition
Morris
0 434 91266 2   £14.95

Using the Amstrad PCW9512
John Campbell
0 7506 0169 8   £12.95

DESKTOP PUBLISHING

Ventura 4.0 for Windows
John Campbell
0 7506 0632 0   £14.95

Pagemaker 4.0 for Windows
Alan Balfe
0 7506 0634 7   £14.95

Corel Draw 2.0
John Cambell & Marion Pye
0 7506 0503 0   £14.95

PROGRAMMING

Using Quick Basic 4.5
Stephen Morris
0 7506 0220 1   £14.95

Visual Basic
Stephen Morris
0 7506 0633 9   £14.95

Programming in G-W Basic
P K McBride
0 7506 0256 2   £14.95

Also of Interest

A series of handy, inexpensive, **pocket size reference books** to be kept by the computer and used every day. Their size makes them an ideal 'travelling' companion as well. **All titles are hardback.**

Newnes MS-DOS Pocket Book
2nd Edition
Second edition
Ian Sinclair

Over 110,000 copies sold of the 1st edition This best-selling title has been enlarged and updated to include material on version 5.0.

7506 0328 3   £9.95

Newnes MAC Users Pocket Book
Steve Heath

A handy all-round reference book for users of any MAC machine.

7506 0083 7   £12.95

Newnes PC Printers Pocket Book
Stephen Morris

Will be invaluable to anyone who has a program that requires them to set to their own printer codes, anyone having a problem with their printer or wants to use some of its more exotic facilities.

7506 0197 3   £12.95

Newnes C Pocket Book
Conor Sexton

Covers in as succinct a manner as possible the C language as defined by the ANSI standard.

07506 0221 X   £12.95

Newnes Data Communications Pocket Book
Second edition
Michael Tooley

Will be invaluable for anyone involved with the interconnection of computer systems: from technicians and engineers to managers involved in the purchase of datacomms equipment.

0 7506 0427 1   £10.95

Newnes PC Users Pocket Book
Jim Reid

Based on the IBM PC range, including 286, 386 and 486 models. Will appeal to all programmers and computer enthusiasts.

0 7506 0085 3   £12.95

Newnes Hard Disk Pocket Book
2nd Edition
Mike Allen & Tim Kay

A comprehensive guide to hard disk, covering every aspect from the disk manufacture, the drives and their components, organization, utilities and data safety.

0 7506 0470 0   £12.95

Newnes 8086 Family Pocket Book
Ian Sinclair

A portable guide to the Intel family of 16/32 bit processors. Covers the 8086, 8088, 80186, 80188, 80286, 80386 and 80486 types.

0 434 91872 5   £10.95

Newnes Windows 3 Pocket Book
Ian Sinclair

Features the use of Windows 3 with MS-DOS 5, a combination which will be increasingly common as users change over to version 5.0

0 7506 0347 X   £12.95

Newnes Unix Pocket Book
Heath

There are many UNIX books around but none that contain all the information necessary to get the best out of the system - This book does just that.

0 7506 0391 7   £12.95

Newnes Computer Engineers Pocket Book
Third edition
Michael Tooley

An invaluable compendium of facts, circuits and data that makes an indispensible guide to the designer, service engineer and all those interested in computer and microsystems.

0 7506 0372 0   £12.95

Related Titles...

The Chaos Cookbook
Joe Pritchard

Examines chaos theory in a much more practical way than other books and includes type-in-and-go listings which even the initiated will appreciate.

0 7506 0304 6   £16.95

Designing your systems with Smartware II
Martin Gandolf & Michael Hicks

Introduces the concepts and principles of system design and shows what must be considered when developing your own system using Smartware II. Essential for all users of the popular and powerful integrated package.

0 7506 0425 5   £19.95

Wordstar Professional Handbook Version 4
John Campbell

Provides a source of basic information while leaning and then as a handbook of practical tips and memory joggers once you have mastered the essentials

0 434 90242 X   £22.50

Using Pagemaker 3.0 on the IBM-compatible AT
Alan Balfe
Complete with appendices covering associated programs, this guide will allow you to realise and master the power and potential of PageMaker 3.0

0 434 91318 9   £16.95

Using Ventura 2.0
John Campbell

Contents: Making a Start; The basic tools; What you do - and how; Fine tuning - getting the details right. John Campbell is an experienced trainer and hasthe knack of covering the ground in the right sequence so that one piece of information leads naturally to another.

0 434 90272 1   £16.95

Lotus Symphony 2.0 Handbook
Stephen Morris

The aim of this book is to show you how to get the most out of Symphony 2. The emphasis is on practical applications, with examples drawn from many different aspects of business.

0 434 91302 2   £17.50

Using SuperCalc 5.0 in Business Spreadsheets in 3 dimensions
P K McBride
INCLUDES FREE DISK

Explores and explains the huge potential of the system with the 3d capabilities very much in mind. The free disk contains copies of the sheets used in the book and blank sheets ready to be tailored to your needs.

0 434 91308 1   £27.50

Hypertalk and Hypertext Programming the Interface graphic in the Macintosh and Windows 3 with Hypercard 2 Plus
A E Stanley

Presents the fundamental working of GUI in the context of object-orientated programming tools for the end user. All command/functions and uses of Hypertalk and Hypertext are covered.

0 7506 0500 6   £19.95

Wordcraft 6 Handbook
Sue Horrocks

Contents: System requirement; Operating system; Installing WordCraft WordCarft basicsl Modes of operation Menus; Basic text controls and commands; Using text; Designing and editing a report using advanced features; Spell check; Printing; Using images in text; Troubleshooting.

0 434 91324 3   £30.0

Macintosh Business Book
Joe Sudwarts

Written by an internationally known expert, this book covers everything from initial hardware and software selections to the effective use of networking, information exchange and communication for the Mac User in business and coporation environment.

0 7506 0502 2   £21.

Scanning and Printing Perfect Pictures with Desktop Publishing
Peter & Anton Kammermeier

Provides all DTP users who want to integrate photos in their documents with practical hints and numerical values for image editing and printing. Aimed at the beginner as well as the professional user.

7506 0539 1 £36.99

Servicing Personal Computers
Third Edition
Michael Tooley

The revised and enlarged version of this bestselling book contains a new chapter on servicing 68000-based microcomputers. It has also been updated throughout and contains many new photographs and diagrams.

0 7506 0374 7 £25.00

The Scanner Handbook
A complete guide to the use and applications of desktop scanners
Stephen Beale & James Cavuoto

An authoritative and informative guide to selecting, installing and using a desktop scanner. Offers practical tips and indispensable advice throughout.

0 434 90069 9 £19.95

Wordperfect for Windows:
A Guide to Professional Document Production
Andrew Glynn Smail

Considers how to achieve predetermined goals in document production, rather than merely acquainting the reader with the use of the functions of the program.

0 7506 0541 3 £19.95

Order Form

Title	ISBN	Price	Qty	Total
			UK & Surface Postage & packing	£2.00
			Grand Total	

❑ Please send Airmail (extra costs will be charged)
❑ Cheques/Postal Order enclosed
   (Cheques should be made payable to Butterworth-Heinemann Ltd)
❑ Credit Card ❑ Access ❑ American Express ❑ Visa ❑ Diner

❑❑❑❑❑❑❑❑❑❑❑❑❑❑ Expiry date _____

Name _____ Company _____

* Address _____

Tel No _____ Signature _____ Date _____

* If paying by credit card use address shown on your credit card statement.

Please return this form to:
Alice Scott-Taylor, Butterworth-Heinemann Ltd, Linacre House, Jordan Hill, Oxford OX2 8D
Alternatively, phone our distribution centre direct on 0983-410511, quoting ref: B29
(Please have credit card details ready) **PRICES ARE SUBJECT TO CHANGE**

Best Selling Amstrad PCW Titles from Butterworth-Heinemann

Using the Amstrad PCW 9512
John Campbell

Designed for the relative beginner, this book has over 170 pages describing how to understand and use all the facilities of the Amstrad PCW 9512. The clear text and screen shots take you step by step through using the hardware, using discs and files, mailshots creating documents, page layout, CP/M and the printed page. In fact, everything you are likely to need for a successful future.

"An excellent book... for the beginner on the PCW 9512 - easy to follow and full of sound advice. And where do you go eight months later when you begin to feel the urge to widen your computer horizons?... Where else but `Exploiting the Amstrad PCW 9512'"
PCW Plus Magazine

£12.95   ISBN 0 7506 0169 8

Exploiting the Amstrad PCW 9512
John Campbell & Marion Pye

For more experienced users who want to use their machine as a full blown computer, this book not only examines the PCW as a word processor with LocoScript but also explores the range of other programs available. 300 plus pages with detailed information on LocoScript, LocoMail, CP/M, LocoFile, dBaseII, SuperCalc 2 and Mini Office Professional.

"... it would make an invaluable aid to any 9512 owner... The book contains a great deal of practical information which is laid out in a helpful and concise form... I would not hesitate to recommend it to any newcomer as being excellent value for money."
Newsletter to the Lawyers' PCW Club

£14.95   ISBN 0 7506 0075 6

Order Form

Title	ISBN	Price	Qty	Total
Using the Amstrad PCW 9512	0 7506 0169 8	£12.95		
Exploiting the Amstrad PCW 9512	0 7506 0075 6	£14.95		
		UK & Surface Postage & packing		£2.00
			Grand Total	

☐ Please send Airmail (extra costs will be charged)
☐ Cheques/Postal Order enclosed
  (Cheques should be made payable to Butterworth-Heinemann Ltd)
☐ Credit Card   ☐ Access   ☐ American Express   ☐ Visa   ☐ Diners

☐☐☐☐ ☐☐☐☐ ☐☐☐☐ ☐☐☐☐ Expiry date _____

Name _____   Company _____

* Address _____

_____

Tel No _____ Signature _____ Date _____
* If paying by credit card use address shown on your credit card statement.

Please return this form to:
Alice Scott-Taylor, Butterworth-Heinemann Ltd, Linacre House, Jordan Hill, Oxford OX2 8DP.
Alternatively, phone our distribution centre direct on 0983-410511, quoting ref: B2901
Please have credit card details ready.

THE BEST SELLING MAGAZINE FOR THE
AMSTRAD PCW
8256 ● 8512 ● 9512 ● 9256 ● 9512+

PCW PLUS

Future Publishing is a totally independent company and the largest publisher of computer magazines in the country. Every one is a clear market leader and *PCWPlus,* which has been running for over 5 years, is no exception.

PCWPlus has over 90 pages every month totally dedicated to the Amstrad PCW and is produced by *a* team of highly dedicated PCW users who have your best interests at heart. As a consequence, *PCWPlus* consistently delivers what the readership wants - unbiased reviews, informed features, and tutorials that offer practical step-by-step help.

Every month in PCW Plus, you will flnd regular sections on spreadsheets, databases, DTP packages and public domain software. All the latest hardware and software is ruthlessly reviewed; you don't just get technical data, you get the complete lowdown on a product's usefulness and value for money. This allows you to make genuinely informed purchasing decisions - avoiding costly errors and saving frustration and money.

In addition, there are articles on Protext, Mini Office Professional and at least five pages covering the entire range of Locomotive's software . . . plus practical tips on programming and DIY hardware maintenance

You get all these benefits when you subscribe:

Your copy is guaranteed - avoid the disapointment of missing an issue

Your copy is delivered to your door at no extra charge - save yourself the time and trouble of having to go and flnd your copy every month.

You save money- subscribe now using the special form provided and you will save 22p an issue on the newsstand price!

You gain access to special promotional offers - at exclusive prices.

You protect yourself against inflation - the price you pay now is held for the duration of your subscription Even if the cover price goes up you don't pay a single penny more.

You have our cast-iron guarantee. You can cancel your subscription at any time in the future and we will refund you for all unmailed issues - no quibbles.

Save over 25p an issue when you subscribe to PCW PLUS

YES! PLEASE ENTER MY SUBSCRIPTION FOR 12 ISSUES OF PCW PLUS AT THE MONEY-SAVING PRICE TICKED BELOW!

☐ UK £23.75   ☐ Europe £40.10   ☐ Rest of World £54.75

TO ENSURE YOUR MAGAZINE ARRIVES QUICKLY AND UNDAMAGED, ALL OVERSEAS SUBSCRIPTIONS ARE SENT AIRMAIL. THESE COSTS ARE INCLUDED IN THE ABOVE PRICES.

MY METHOD OF PAYMENT IS tick your choice

☐ **Visa**

☐ **Access**

No ☐☐☐☐ ☐☐☐☐ ☐☐☐☐ ☐☐☐☐

EXPIRY DATE ☐☐☐☐

☐ **Cheque** MAKE PAYABLE TO FUTURE PUBLISHING LTD

Name _____

Address _____

_____

Post Code _____

Signature _____

SEND THIS COUPON (TOGETHER WITH YOUR CHEQUE IF APPLICABLE) IN AN ENVELOPE TO:
PCW PLUS, Freepost, Somerton, TA11 7BR
THIS COUPON IS VALID UNTIL 31 DEC 1992   PCW/0192/Book